Social justice and intercultural education:
an open ended dialogue

Social justice and intercultural education:
an open ended dialogue

Edited by Ghazala Bhatti,
Chris Gaine, Francesca Gobbo
and Yvonne Leeman

Trentham Books
Stoke on Trent, UK and Sterling, USA

Trentham Books Limited
Westview House   22883 Quicksilver Drive
734 London Road   Sterling
Oakhill   VA 20166-2012
Stoke on Trent   USA
Staffordshire
England ST4 5NP

© 2007 Ghazala Bhatti, Chris Gaine, Francesca Gobbo and Yvonne Leeman

First published 2007

British Library Cataloguing-in-Publication Data
A catalogue record for this book is available from the British Library

ISBN-13: 978 1 85856 403 6

Cover photograph: Roma children in Debrecin, Hungary by Ghazala Bhatti

Designed and typeset by Trentham Print Design Ltd, Chester and printed in Great Britain by Hobbs the Printers Ltd, Hampshire.

Contents

Acknowledgements

The Social Justice and Intercultural Education Network would like to acknowledge the support it has received over the years through the interest and active participation of many friends and colleagues. It wishes in particular to extend grateful thanks for this publication which was provided by the Development Cooperation Ireland, during the ECER 2005 Conference in Dublin.

Introduction

This volume brings together selected papers presented at ECER 2004 in Crete and ECER 2005 in Dublin. It is one of the few attempts to disseminate a Europe-wide reflexive approach to intercultural education and social justice which goes beyond merely presenting and discussing national policies. It focuses instead on contexualising empirical work within the landscape of a changing Europe, forcing researchers to interact creatively with the challenging perspectives embedded in the data itself.

From the inception of Network 7 at ECER in 1996 to 2006, issues presented here have held their significance for researchers across Europe. This is both because the challenge of holding on to the value encapsulated in the term 'social justice' as seen through the eyes of researchers working in different countries retains its descriptive and analytical power, and also because the challenges debated here have yet to be met and problems have yet to be resolved.

The term 'intercultural' has a variety of meanings, depending on different national contexts and the policy trajectories in each of them. In some circles in countries such as England and Sweden it is associated with an outdated idea, where the very notion of 'multicultural' education is seen to have had its day. It has been discredited because it is seen not to add any new meaning to public discourse about issues of equity. The same logic is then extended by association to 'intercultural' education. In the Netherlands the ideal of a multicultural society has officially come to an end. There citizenship education for integration has been used to replace intercultural education.

However, there are circles of scholars and teachers who value the concept of intercultural education to describe and analyse inter-cultural challenges. Thus 'intercultural' education continues to be used. In Greece and Italy inter-cultural stands for valuable communication and a sincere attempt to understand diversity within the fast changing landscape of shifting identities and new alignments. It symbolises hope and an active stance against growing inequality. This explains the open-ended nature of the title of this book. We are working in a contested terrain which continues to grow in complexity while retaining the promise of a resolution – or many. So it is exciting to be researching the field now.

The Social Justice and Intercultural Education network came into being during discussions at ECER in the University of Seville over a decade ago, when Ghazala Bhatti and Joanna McPake set about creating a network which would help bring together researchers interested in exploring contested issues concerning justice, ethnicity, social inequality, gender and equity. Since then the network has grown. It has four convenors and over 90 people have chosen to present their papers to researchers and colleagues at the network over the years. This edited collection presents a flavour of the themes, which continue to provoke debate and discussion. The chapters have been clustered in four sections.

Teachers, teaching and social justice
The three chapters in this section are concerned with the interplay between identity, ethnicity, diversity and achievement.

Mary Clarke and Sheelagh Drudy's research, concerned with a post-graduate initial teacher education programme in Ireland, explores student teachers' attitudes to social justice. A high level of economic growth has made Ireland attractive for inward migration to a society which had been relatively homogeneous. Hostility to black communities, Roma and Travellers, and refugees and asylum seekers has intensified. The chapter describes the implementation and evaluation of a programme designed to incorporate global awareness, social justice and deeper understanding of diversity and to increase student experience of active and inclusive teaching and learning. Even though student teachers were generally enthusiastic and committed to teaching about diversity and global issues, they lacked confidence in their ability to teach what they considered controversial or difficult issues. The analysis of student teachers' reflections in this study illustrates clearly the challenges involved in the promotion of critical reflection in teaching social justice and the praxis that supports it in initial teacher education.

The chapter by Chris Derrington and Sally Kendall is concerned with Gypsy Traveller children's under-achievement and limited access to secondary education in England. Children's entitlement to education and the dissonance between the culture and value systems of home and school are discussed. Teachers' low expectations about Traveller students' attendance, combined with a high incidence of bullying, was partly responsible for low participation rates. Gender was an important factor when considering school attendance. The desire to maintain the Traveller culture and language was evident through the prevalence of Romani, Gaelic or 'Traveller language'. It is suggested that 'too much emphasis on cultural expectations can lead to a theory of cultural pathology in which other related factors may be insufficiently considered'. Many Gypsy Traveller students have to deal with cultural dissonance, racism and social or cultural alienation and this affects young people's development of identity and self-concept. The researchers emphasise that individuals who feel socially and culturally isolated are unlikely to reach their full potential within such an environment.

The chapter by Ghazala Bhatti is based on interviews of aspiring teachers studying for a Post Graduate Certificate in Education, particularly those who choose to teach information and communication technology (ICT). Almost half the intake in a typical year comprises people from diverse backgrounds who are highly motivated and interested in teaching, whereas other subjects rarely attract and retain similar students. Some of the reasons were predictable. However, unsolicited information reflected broader social issues facing secondary school teachers, such as: experiences of their own schooling, family members as positive role models, the position of minority ethnic teachers in secondary schools, achievement in their own careers and experiences of racism and religious affiliation. Most participants related learning to teach with self-discovery and self-knowledge; it pointed the way to 'survival with respect'. The chapter argues for the training and retention of teachers from a diversity of backgrounds for the benefit of all children.

Intercultural challenges
In the first chapter of the next section Morwenna Griffiths, together with artists Jude Berry, Anna Holt, John Naylor and Philippa Weekes, explore how arts can work for social justice in school, allowing disadvantaged or disaffected children to share a common purpose and move from the margins into the public spaces. The chapter also reflects how this educational and civic goal challenged teachers and researchers to ask how people learn to enter and participate in public spaces. These authors maintain that learning to be able to express themselves will enable children to extend their experience of voice and agency into other public spaces in the school.

Upper secondary school students – most of them of immigrant background – and their relatively low reading skills and literary understanding were the focus of the research on writing and reading in a multicultural classroom, whose positive outcomes and unexpected results are presented by Gitte Holten Ingerslev. The relationship between the students' notions of learning and reading and their school performance in studying Danish literature was taken into account. Their work was significantly improved by a writing task that enhanced the students' reading and interpretation skills as well as their interest in literature. This invites readers to reflect on the feelings and life experiences of young immigrants in Denmark and on schools' lack of attention to students' varied approaches to learning and education.

In 'Teaching teachers cooperative learning: an intercultural challenge', Francesca Gobbo presents her experience of training teachers for cooperative learning, which developed into a classroom experiment that challenged both the teachers' professional identity and the researcher's expectations. She used reflective conversations with the teachers to understand how their everyday classroom competence and prior educational knowledge had interacted with the effort to implement a structured group work such as E. Cohen's Complex Instruction. The author concludes that transmigration or dissemination of innovative ideas in the field of school education cannot but encounter, and take into account, the web of local educational practices and theories.

Constructing identities

The three chapters in this section are all about identities and their boundaries and how these are negotiated by people in different contexts. The contribution from Ann-Sofie Holm and Elisabet Öhrn in Sweden starts from the argument that 'femininities are said to be more diverse than masculinities because of differences in pressure to subordinate to hegemonic forms of gender'. From fieldwork in two secondary schools, one fairly homogenous and the other more ethnically mixed, they unravel the way some girls learn to 'do gender' in relation to established roles, and explore how some immigrant boys negotiate their way through the possible ways open to them of being boys.

Indra Dewan's chapter moves us up the age range to adult women in education, and how her mixed-heritage interviewees negotiate the essentialised expectations they encounter: who they expected to identify with and the stereotypes they have to resist. How these women switch between discourses about mixed heritage, race, and individual striving and educational achievement is fascinating. As Dewan observes, 'one of the main theoretical challenges which these findings pose is how to reconcile 'raced' and 'individualist' notions of self.'

If Indra Dewan's chapter provides a close up of the construction of identity in process, Chris Gaine's stands back, discussing how British young people identify ethnically and racially when asked to do so anonymously on an educational website. This is not about classroom processes but about context, about the way young people locate themselves in a pervasive discourse in Britain about these aspects of identity. The chapter is part of a wider debate that asks: how do young people perceive ethnicity and should curricula engage with this?

Sketching pictures for improvement

The chapters in this section sketch pictures of inequality and of intercultural tensions in education. These pictures aim to provide the knowledge required to improve policies. Amy Garett Dikkers focuses on research and theory around issues related to the improvement of immigrant education and correlates these findings with education for Roma and Sinti children. She studied four different programmes for Roma education in Germany and concluded that addressing issues of language, socialisation differences, attendance and parental involvement are key for acceptance of the programmes by the parents. What is needed is an alignment of the implementation needs of policymakers with the desires of Roma families. She stresses that social integration with German students and students of other immigrant groups is beneficial to the growth of the children and their future hopes for employment and integrated life in Germany.

Linda Croxford looks at changes in young people's experiences of schooling. It focuses upon social class differences between the education systems of England and Scotland, the key difference being the extent of comprehensive school provision. The chapter examines levels of attainment and perceptions of school experiences to prepare pupils for life after school. There is strong evidence that the attainment gap associated with social class has diminished in Scotland. However, it is difficult to judge whether changing patterns of inequality are influenced by educational or broader national differences.

Hester Radstake and Yvonne Leeman have studied intercultural education and tense situations in ethnically diverse classrooms in the Netherlands. Their chapter reports the results of a national survey into tense situations teachers experience in mixed classes and how they react. The authors state that noticing tense situations and reacting to them are important teaching competences in ethnically diverse classes. Teachers can assess situations in different ways: as an expression of problem behaviour by the pupils or as an indication of inadequate inclusion of diversity in the class, school and society. They conclude that professionality is at stake. Teachers should be alert to the significance of their own role regarding social justice and cultural diversity.

Thematically, then, there are interconnections between the strands presented in this book. They signal to teachers, educational researchers and policy makers that intercultural education requires awareness of the rapidly changing socio-cultural landscape and sensitivity to the fact that social justice and equity issues concerns both 'us' and 'them', however defined these terms are). The ways in which the researchers and the researched have negotiated the space from which to highlight the main issues shows a diversity of approaches and interpretations. It also shows how the voices, hopes and dilemmas of the researched can give important indications for a truly intercultural interaction. The readers' engagements with the texts presented here will help initiate new interconnections. We hope the dialogue will continue.

Section I
Teachers, teaching and social justice

1

Social justice in initial teacher education: student teachers' reflections on praxis

Marie Clarke and Sheelagh Drudy

School of Education and Life Long Learning,
University College Dublin, Ireland

Introduction

As one of the fastest changing societies in Europe, the Republic of Ireland is a valuable site in which to examine the challenges facing teacher education in terms of providing social justice and intercultural education. This chapter explores the findings from a study conducted with a group of student teachers in Ireland who were involved in teaching a development module containing a social justice dimension. During the decade to 2006 Ireland enjoyed high levels of economic growth. Formerly a relatively homogeneous society, by 2002, 7.1 per cent of the population of Ireland had a nationality other than Irish (CSO, 2005). This was due to the increase in net migration (inward migration less outward migration) between 1996-2002 of 26 per cent.

Data indicate newly emergent trends arising from these changes. For example, the Equality Authority has reported that 'race' now counts for the largest category of the case files under the Employment Equality Acts (Equality Authority, 2006). A recent review of attitudes to minority ethnic groups in all existing surveys in Ireland

(EUMC RAXEN3, 2002) indicates that hostility has increased and is particularly evident towards groups such as black people, Roma, Travellers, refugees and asylum seekers. In the context of such changes, issues of social justice are present at school level – particularly concerning attitudes to poverty, diversity, racism and discrimination. These findings provide the backdrop against which children from minority ethnic backgrounds experience school and against which student teachers have their first experience of teaching practice. In this study student teachers' attitudes to issues of social justice were explored.

Once their initial attitudes and values towards social justice issues were established, the study concentrated on how the student teachers prepared and reflected on the lessons they had delivered. A number of themes emerged which are of central importance in teacher education. These include the tendency for student teachers to focus mainly on their pupils' responses rather than on their own actions or on wider structural issues. This is a challenge for teacher education because student teachers must go beyond a focus on pupil responses if they are to achieve the capacity to reflect critically on issues of social justice.

The study indicated that many student teachers find teaching material with a social justice dimension problematic, particularly in classes where pupil backgrounds, abilities and social stratification are diverse. The findings also suggest that the majority of student teachers did not reflect critically on social justice issues in their own classroom praxis.

Social justice and development education

Social justice is itself a contested concept (Novak, 2000). In the field of education social justice is explained using various theoretical models relating to distribution, recognition and redistribution (Lynch and Lodge, 2002). Sen (2002) advances a 'capabilities' approach within social justice – a broad normative framework for the evaluation of individual wellbeing, social arrangements, the design of policies and proposals about social change in society. Skills and personality traits are also considered, and people's thoughts, emotions, meaning and action (Nussbaum 2003). The theoretical approach on which the present research is built is informed by these frameworks.

Development education takes an approach to learning and teaching based upon individual rights, active participation, the evaluation of change and the empowerment of people to become actively involved in their own futures (Leach, 1994). Development education can thus be located within a social justice capabilities model, which promotes an active approach to learning. This attracts many teachers to the subject. While reflection is encouraged, the focus is generally on the methodology. It is therefore important that teacher education integrates theories of social justice, development and education with approaches to reflection so that beginning teachers might be enabled to explore these areas in the context of their praxis.

Reflective practice

Zeichner (2001) suggests that a central part of teachers' reflections should be informed by how their everyday actions challenge or support various oppressions and injustices related to social class, race, gender, sexual preference, religion and so forth. Yet there is little consensus on exact definitions of reflection, its application within learning, teaching and even teacher education (Brookfield, 1990, 1995; Grimmett *et al*, 1990; Munby and Russell, 1993; Newman, 1999; Phelan, 1997; Schön, 1983).

Reflective practice requires a conscious, systematic, deliberate process of framing and re-framing classroom practice in light of the consequences of actions, democratic principles, educational beliefs, values and the preferred visions which teachers bring to the teaching-learning event (Serafini, 2003, 2001). As teacher education continues to promote reflective practice, teachers face many challenges in relation to the praxis dimension of reflection (Serafini, 2003, 2001). Research (Shannon and Crawford, 1998; Mitchell and Weber, 1996) shows that although student teachers appreciate the potential value of reflective practice in theory, many of them choose not to reflect on their practice constructively and critically.

Tabachnick and Zeichner (1991) identified four approaches to understanding reflective practice. The 'academic' approach is concerned with pedagogical content and knowledge. The 'social efficiency' approach is concerned with skills and techniques. The 'developmentalist' approach focuses on the natural development of the learner and how this should determine the actions of the teacher. The 'social re-constructionist' approach emphasises the school as a social institution which reflects a society based on unjust class, race and gender relations. Each approach directs teachers' reflections to particular aspects of teaching practice – the representation of subject matter, children's thinking, the social context, or to particular teaching strategies suggested by research on teaching. No approach is sufficient by itself. We argue that Tabachnik and Zeichner's categorical framework provides a valuable construct for analysing the reflections of the student teachers in this study.

The study

This research, conducted with a single year student cohort on a postgraduate initial teacher education programme in Ireland, used quantitative and qualitative methodologies. It entailed implementing and evaluating a programme designed to incorporate global awareness, social justice and deeper understandings about diversity across all areas of special methods (didactics) in the programme, in order to increase student experience of active and inclusive teaching and learning. Development education was the focal point of this work. The research programme involved:

- designing and implementing a programme on diversity, human rights, social justice and global awareness through workshops focused on several class based activities that could be implemented
- the design and implementation of a pre-programme questionnaire to measure pre-existing attitudes and values towards social justice, diversity and human rights issues, and preferred types of classroom practice
- post-programme evaluations by the student teachers
- content analysis of lesson plans involving themes on diversity, human rights and social justice
- content analysis of student teacher reflections on these lessons after they were taught
- focus group interviews.

6

This chapter focuses on the content analysis of the post-lesson reflections. Content analysis is a useful tool for investigating the thematic content of documents (Sarantakos, 1993; Stemler, 2001). It involves systematic text analysis which preserves the advantages of quantitative content analysis and further develops it to qualitative interpretation (Mayring, 2000). This technique was well suited to the study of post-lesson reflections where the context and boundaries of analysis were clearly defined. It helped to provide a range of qualitative insights.

Profile and attitudes

The student cohort was fairly homogenous. The gender balance of 22 per cent male and 78 per cent female is close to the national pattern for entrants to second level teaching (Drudy *et al*, 2005). Of 78 per cent of BA graduates who completed the questionnaire, there were 10.2 per cent science graduates (somewhat lower than the course average of 16 per cent over the five year period 2001-2005), 3.1 per cent were commerce graduates, and 7 per cent were business studies graduates. Most respondents were under 25 years of age. 20.3 per cent were between 25 and 34 years and 4 per cent were between 45-54 years in age. Most – 64.3 per cent – of the respondents had no previous teaching experience. The rest had previous unqualified teaching experience.

The attitudinal findings of this study (Clarke and Drudy, 2006) showed variations in orientation to social justice and diversity issues among the student teachers. Although a relationship between their attitudes to diversity and their teaching goals was not established, their preferred teaching strategies were largely conservative and traditional. This suggests that they might not be well placed to meet the needs of students in diverse classrooms appropriately. Older students and those teaching subjects with a high diversity, social justice and global awareness content were more positively orientated to diversity (*ibid*). It was important to establish previous experience before exploring how the student teachers planned and reflected on the lessons they delivered.

Post-lesson reflections

The lesson plans and post-lesson reflections were presented as part of their teaching practice portfolios. Copies were submitted separately to the researchers for analysis.

The reflections as documented were transcribed and categorised. The post-lesson reflections were categorised according to the approaches identified by Tabachnick and Zeichner (1991). A number of lesson plans were submitted which had no reflections and some lesson plans had not been implemented at the time of portfolio submission. As a result they had no reflections attached. The results of this analysis are presented in Table 1.

Table 1: Most prominent themes in reflections on lessons taught

Reflective theme	Frequency	%
Social efficiency approach Activities in the classroom	34	24.0
Developmentalist approach Development of learners and actions of the teacher	100	70.0
Social reconstructionist approach Social justice themes within development education	8	6.0
Total reflections	142	100.0
Note: no reflections 11; lessons not delivered, 3.		

The details and nature of the reflections in the four categories are set out below, discussed under the headings of academic, social efficiency, developmentalist and social reconstructionist approaches. The reflections presented in this chapter are representative of what the students submitted. None of the post-lesson reflections could be categorised solely under the academic approach. Most focused on the pupils – particularly their reactions to the material covered in class.

Social efficiency approach to reflection

The student teachers who adopted the social efficiency approach focused on the technical aspects of their classes – the way the activities worked in the classroom context. Class activities that featured prominently in the lessons included paired work, brainstorming, group work, videos, specific development education activities, photographs, debates, songs and simulations.

Many student teachers in the study employed the activities that they had themselves been exposed to in the workshops. Classroom management emerged in the reflections as an issue, in particular the noise levels associated with the activities and with maintaining control in class:

> The exercise at the beginning of the class was very good. However it was sometimes hard to maintain control while the drama was in process some of the things that the girls were asking the other girls to do was outrageous and involved a lot of noise.

> A lesson like this proves the effectiveness of active participation by the students, the auction was great fun but very noisy.

It was clear from the reflections that these student teachers were focused on the methodologies involved in delivering these classes. Leach (1994) would agree that the activities in the classroom take precedence over reflections on the issues involved. The data also indicated evidence of student teachers' awareness and concern about their pupils' progress and viewpoints. This was especially reflected in reflections that had a more developmentalist approach.

Developmentalist approach to reflection

The majority of the 'developmentalist' reflections consisted of an exclusive focus on pupils' reactions to the material covered in class. These included: pupil enjoyment of the lessons, the active participation of pupils in the lessons, and pupils' reactions to the topics covered. Terms such as 'actively engaged', 'interested', 'contributed well', 'excellent recall' and 'participation by all members of the class' emerged consistently in these reflections. Pupils' enjoyment of the class was typified by the following reflections:

> I think that this case was beneficial for the pupils and it was different from the normal class lessons. Everyone had a valid point to make.

> Students were very interested in the activities as opposed to the formal geometry expected. The activity based lessons appealed to the students.

> Students thoroughly enjoyed this approach in their class. They loved being able to walk around the class and the informal atmosphere. They took the activity very seriously and they listened attentively to the statements, the weaker students had a lot to contribute.

The student teachers felt that their pupils enjoyed the lessons because they saw them as different to their other lessons. This suggests that the student teachers in this study did not regularly employ active methodologies. Some evidence of a relatively low level of use of active learning methodologies also emerged from the questionnaire data, where formal class lessons predominated as the preferred approach to teaching (Clarke and Drudy, 2006).

Pupil responses and the development of pupils' awareness and understanding about development was seen as part of the natural progress of the learner. Phrases such as 'taken aback', 'shock', 'change in outlook', 'surprise' and 'outrage' described the reactions of pupils to the issues arising in the lessons. The terms 'honesty' and 'maturity' were consistently applied to pupils. For example:

> Pupils were taken aback when I put the facts and the figures on the board. I let the pupils do the worksheets in pairs and I was impressed with the differences they came up with.

The pupils' reaction to inequalities was considered to be noteworthy – especially with regard to raising awareness of the differences between how much people were paid to make goods and the amount pupils paid to buy the same goods:

> Students were very surprised that so many of what they considered commonplace goods came from all around the world. As a result of the approach taken there was a fairly long list of goods on the board. Students were initially amazed and then outraged by the difference in how much the person who made the goods got paid

and how much they bought them for. The students were much more aware of the world outside of Ireland by the end of the class.

According to a student teacher, pupils were also very interested in the differences between 'the Third World and us [Irish]'.

Pupils acknowledged that they themselves labelled people but said they did not do it deliberately. Some admitted to having carried out injustices and acknowledged that they did not realise the full impact of their actions until they themselves had a similar experience:

> Pupils really enjoyed today's exercise and were very mature with regard to labelling people. They did however admit to doing it but claimed that it was not deliberate. They simply didn't think, and labelled people according to what they hear from other people.

> They were really honest and open in their discussion and some admitted to having carried out injustices not realising the effect their behaviour was having on others until the tables were turned. It was a very successful lesson.

It is clear from these reflections that the student teachers believed that their pupils actively participated and enjoyed the classes which focused on social justice issues. Pupils made connections between subject matter and the themes developed. The pupils' reactions to many of the topics demonstrated that they were interested in such issues. They showed awareness of inequalities and of unfairness in the treatment of others. The student teachers' reflections indicate that most of them concentrated on pupil reactions to the lessons. The data did not provide any insight into the student teachers' personal views about social justice. There was an absence of critical reflection about the lessons.

These student teachers viewed the role of the teacher as an observer of pupils' reactions and progress. These reflections indicated that these student teachers possessed a traditional view of teaching, which may be described as 'preconceived understandings about teachers and students' roles in the classroom' Cordingley (1999). Few student teachers actually reflected within the social reconstructionist approach.

Social reconstructionist approaches to reflection

Only eight lesson plans contained reflections that specifically highlighted unjust class, race and gender relations. Of these, most reflected on their own feelings in relation to conducting lessons on development education:

> This was the most enjoyable class I have ever taught. The pupils were able to recall each of the people looked at in the video and were disgusted at the dangers involved in getting to safety. The board game worked really well and their opinions had changed by the end of the lesson! I was aware that there is a little girl from Afghanistan in the class so I had to be careful.

The feelings articulated in these reflections included scepticism about the topics and apprehension concerning the subject matter and uncertainty over planning. Some student teachers expressed a sense of fulfilment and personal satisfaction when the lesson was completed.

> I think I really got the girls thinking, it was clear that some of them had never really thought about the issues before we raised them in the lesson.

These student teachers spoke about the need for a fuller integration of social justice themes in the curriculum, as well as of the social context in which development education operates. Those who believed that the syllabi have an important role in raising awareness about social issues expressed concern about the limitations of the current syllabi.

> Regardless of the Junior Cert etc., the human value of developmental education and specifically multicultural awareness goes beyond syllabi and exams.

> Groups worked well, learning objectives were achieved in that students had a less insular view at the end of the lesson and were more aware of development issues. Overall an important topic to teach but the syllabus layout does not allow you time to study this in great detail.

One student teacher found that even though the pupils agreed with the concept of having fair trade products, they would not buy them and could not envisage how their role as consumers could make any difference:

> The more I questioned the more it became clear that at this stage these girls agreed with the ideals but wouldn't buy the Fair Trade product and really couldn't see how as individuals, or even as a group, they could make a difference. If this group represents young people in general, then developmental studies definitely need to be integrated more concretely into education.

The concern about curricula limitations suggests a reliance by these student teachers on education as a way of highlighting social justice issues. This also emerged in the attitudinal data from the survey with the students (Clarke and Drudy, 2006). The student teachers did not see their role as teachers as being related to taking an activist approach in relation to social justice issues in their subject areas. As Beijaard *et al* (2004) note, teachers differ in the way they deal with knowledge and attitudes depending on the value they attach to them.

The social context also emerged in reflections focused on development education. Student teachers expressed caution about approaching particular topics, lest they cause offence to foreign national pupils. One student teacher commented:

> I had to be careful with the story from McDonalds as I had an Asian girl in the class but it wasn't a problem and worked out fine. I should have introduced more facts and figures.

One participant wished to avoid discussing development education issues in an Irish context because her pupils came from socially disadvantaged backgrounds. She did not feel equipped to deal with development issues that concerned her pupils directly:

> The pupils in the class come from socially disadvantaged backgrounds, which would have made it un-diplomatic to discuss development issues in Ireland. This belief lead me to believe that the pupils should discuss development issues that do not immediately concern them.

This echoes Holden's (2003) findings. Even though student teachers are generally enthusiastic and committed to teaching about global issues, they lack confidence in their ability to teach what they consider controversial or difficult issues. It also supports the view that many students enter teacher preparation programmes with a thin base of knowledge about their own and other cultural histories and values systems (Cockrell *et al*, 1999).

Conclusions

Smith and Zantioti (1989) have suggested that 'the work of teacher educators is a form of cultural politics in which 'truth' about schools and teaching is produced and contested'. Teacher preparation should facilitate teachers' understanding of their beliefs about race, class, culture and other human diversities (Cockrell *et al*, 1999). The data from this study highlight the challenges of preparing student teachers to teach social justice education. Facilitating what Santos and Nieto (2000) call 'the social and political dimensions of teaching which include inequality, racism, diversity and other forms of structural discrimination' presents difficulties for teacher educators. In this study the heightening of awareness of, and engagement with, social justice and development education issues were part of the specified learning outcomes of the module. Post-programme evaluations by the student teachers at the end of the module were extremely positive. So the low level of social reconstructionist approaches in these students' post-lesson reflections requires explanation. The relative infrequency of reflections specifically on social justice and global inequality indicates the difficulty of bringing together knowledge and awareness with professional practice.

A number of reasons for this can be advanced. The evidence from attitudinal data in the study suggests that the orientation towards social justice issues varied widely among the student teachers. The attitudinal data must be interpreted within the general context of rapid social change in Ireland in the past ten years. The survey data highlighted the fact that the majority of the student teachers relied on traditional teaching strategies in their classrooms. This is similar to the pattern which emerged in Desforges's (1995) US study, which found a pronounced tendency amongst teachers to adhere to 'tried and trusted' broad teaching strategies.

14

The findings from our study also indicate that few student teachers understood social justice from a 'capabilities' approach – i.e. a broad normative framework (Sen, 2002; Nussbaum, 2003). The lessons lacked reflections on issues which are related to social arrangements, and did not show awareness of policies that would bring about change in society. Equally, few of the student teachers considered social justice themes from the perspective of either meaning or action. This may be explained by their inability to relate their knowledge about distribution, recognition and redistribution (Lynch and Lodge, 2002) to their actual classroom praxis.

Reflective practice is a contested area and it is informed by many different approaches and traditions. From this research it emerged that the student teachers in the study mainly reflected within three traditions, the 'social efficiency' the 'developmentalist' and, to a lesser extent, the 'social reconstructionist' approaches, which highlighted their priorities within teaching. A significant number focused on the activities and methodologies involved in teaching the lessons. Most preferred to reflect upon their pupils' responses to social justice issues. They did not see themselves as central to the promotion of social justice within the classroom context. This is partially because their identities as teachers were still based on an initial teacher education programme.

Research also indicates how fragile and tentative the teacher professional identity and professional practice is during initial teacher education and early professional development (Cockrell *et al*, 1999). Where student teachers engaged in reflections that could be categorised within a social reconstructionist approach, teaching controversial material caused difficulty. The student teachers in this study recognised the limitations of current national syllabi to promote social justice at school level, and the inability of their own pupils to respond in an active way to issues of social justice. Within this approach the post lesson reflections did not present what Leach (1994) identified as educational beliefs, values and preferred visions that teachers bring to the teaching and learning event. There was no evidence in their reflections that they themselves, as teachers, would take a more activist approach towards broadening their pupils' viewpoints in any future teaching of such lessons. The analysis of student teachers' reflections in this study illustrates clearly the challenges involved in the promotion of critical reflection in teaching social justice and the praxis that supports it in initial teacher education.

2
Still in school at 16?
Gypsy Traveller students in
English secondary schools

Chris Derrington
Senior Lecturer in Inclusive Education at the
University of Northampton, England
Sally Kendall
Senior Research Officer at the National Foundation
for Educational Research, England

Introduction

Although the education of Gypsy Traveller[1] children in England has developed significantly over the past ten years, issues relating to access and achievement remain matters of concern. The situation is particularly serious for those of secondary school age. Whilst increasing numbers of Gypsy Traveller students are registered in the primary phase, this pattern is not maintained in the secondary sector. Evidence suggests that where Gypsy Traveller students do transfer successfully to secondary school, their attendance is unlikely to continue beyond the age of 14. Official UK reports have described the situation for Gypsy Traveller children of secondary school age as a 'matter of grave concern' (Ofsted, 1996), as they are 'the group most at risk in the education system' (Ofsted, 1999). It has been estimated that as many as 12,000 Gypsy Traveller students are not enrolled in secondary school at all (Ofsted, 2003). Although it should be emphasised that Gypsy Travellers do not constitute a single, homogenous group, a number of significant common cultural influences have been identified in the literature concerning non-participation at secondary level.

Adolescence is traditionally the time when young Gypsy Travellers are expected to help generate income or take on a wider range of domestic responsibilities. Some parents may believe that secondary education has little value or relevance to the Gypsy Traveller lifestyle. Many Gypsy Traveller parents express anxieties about their children's moral, emotional and physical welfare in what they perceive to be a strange and hostile environment, and are fearful that their children will be victimised or subjected to racist taunts. These anxieties are based largely on their own unhappy experiences of school or anecdotal evidence in the community, but their perceptions are supported by a number of research studies. A survey in the north of England for example, found that racist name-calling was the thing Gypsy Traveller children most hated about going to school (Kendrick and Bakewell, 1995). Similarly, Lloyd *et al*'s (1999) study of Gypsy Travellers attending secondary schools in Scotland found that conflict with teachers often led to non-attendance and that much of what schools saw as a lack of discipline, in the form of violent behaviour, may have been in response to racist name-calling.

The study
This chapter reports on the outcomes of a unique longitudinal study, conducted by the authors between 2000 and 2005. It was the first longitudinal study of a group of Gypsy Traveller students, exploring their educational experiences as they transferred and progressed through secondary school in fifteen different local authorities (LAs) throughout England in both urban and rural areas (LAs are geographically based political/administrative units that are responsible for delivering state services, including education, health and social services, to the inhabitants of that area[2]). The study presented the perspectives and insights of the Gypsy Traveller students, their parents, Traveller Education Service (TES) staff and school staff. It is hoped that these perspectives will contribute to, and develop, the

existing body of research in this area. A full report of the findings from the first three years of the study is already in the public domain (Derrington and Kendall, 2004).

A total of 44 Gypsy Traveller students, 24 boys and 20 girls, agreed to take part in the study. Other consenting participants included their parents (mostly mothers and a few fathers); older siblings and other adult relatives; primary and secondary school headteachers; primary school class teachers; heads of year in secondary schools; special educational needs coordinators (SENCOs) in the case of students with special educational needs; form tutors; and TES teachers or support workers. Additional interviews were conducted with learning support assistants and in the case of two students whose parents opted for Education Otherwise (a legal provision allowing parents to arrange education at home) interviews were conducted with their private tutors. Essentially, this was a phenomenological study that aimed to discover what secondary school experience was like for young Gypsy Travellers and to capture a holistic view by involving the range of respondents listed here.

Aims

The purpose of the research was to investigate the complex issue of secondary school attendance and engagement for Gypsy Traveller children and to gain clearer insight into the nature of difficulties that have been identified by researchers and policy makers over the past 40 or so years. Our primary intention was to enable Gypsy Traveller students themselves to broaden our understanding of the complexity of issues surrounding their continued engagement in school beyond the age of 11.

In summary, the research aimed to:

- map and record the educational progress, engagement and experiences of a sample of 44 Gypsy Traveller students over the five year period they progressed through secondary school
- gather and report upon the personal reflections, accounts, expectations and aspirations of the students, their families and teachers

19

- ▓ identify and examine a range of factors which might affect attitudes, levels of achievement and continued involvement in secondary education
- ▓ identify associations and typologies which might support and encourage Gypsy Traveller students to transfer successfully to secondary school and continue to engage in formal education.

Methods

Initial contact and subsequent access to students and their families were facilitated through TES teachers based in the fifteen LAs who acted as gatekeepers. The main criterion for selection was that they were relatively 'settled' in the educational sense. All students in the study had been engaged in primary school education for the preceding two years at least. Although this effectively excluded highly mobile groups, the justification for this criterion was that it would help to distinguish factors associated with secondary school engagement as opposed to access to schooling *per se*. In order to obtain a mix of students, additional criteria for selection included variables such as gender, type of living accommodation, siblings' experiences of secondary school, levels of attainment and parental attitudes.

The final sample therefore comprised 24 boys and 20 girls of whom:

- ▓ 21 lived on authorised local authority owned Gypsy Traveller sites
- ▓ 12 lived in housing
- ▓ 8 lived on authorised privately owned (or rented) plots
- ▓ 3 lived on unauthorised sites (including roadside encampments)

Data were collected in April and November during the first three years of the study. This was to avoid the traditional travelling patterns, to which some Gypsy Traveller families adhere during the summer months. The first round of interviews took place when students were in their final year of primary school (aged 11) and the final round of data collection took place in the summer of 2005 once the students reached the statutory school leaving age of 16.

Semi-structured interview schedules were designed within a thematic framework that took account of: attitudes, achievement, identity, involvement and participation, relationships, practical barriers and expectations and aspirations. Each year, separate face-to-face interviews were conducted with the students, one or both of their parents, and at least two teachers from their current school, typically their form tutor and a member of the senior management team. The teacher interviews focused on the progress and development of the young people involved in the study. Interviews were tape recorded and later transcribed. Between interviews, additional interim data were collected using short proformas that were sent to schools and TESs to obtain quantitative information such as attendance figures, confirmation of standardised attainment test results (SATs) and numbers of Gypsy Traveller students in each year group. All the young people and their parents gave permission for us to collect these additional data from their schools and TES workers carried out informal interviews with students and parents as part of their usual monitoring role.

Interviews with parents and students were usually held in their own homes, although some of the students elected to be interviewed at school. In some cases, student interviews took place in the presence of a parent but no teachers were present during student interviews. Interviews with teachers and headteachers were held separately in schools, and interviews with TES staff took place either in schools or TES offices.

Although all efforts were made to ensure objectivity, the fact that we, the researchers, are not Gypsy Travellers was bound to influence the responses of the pupils and parents. Despite the fact that interviews were conducted in an informal manner, and the consistency of the researcher/participant relationship over the five-year period, it is likely that some of the responses were influenced by the experience of being influenced by a *gauje* (non-Gypsy Traveller) involved in education. Similarly, multiple realities exist in all qualitative studies and despite striving for objective interpretation of the data, this will almost certainly have been influenced by our inability to get inside the participants' life-world and, in particular, the Gypsy Traveller culture.

In total, over 400 interviews were conducted and transcribed over the course of the study. Data were input into a data analysis software programme using a system of coding based on the thematic framework which guided data collection as outlined above. The data were analysed using an approach that was informed by interpretative phenomenological analysis (IPA). This has been described by Smith and Osborn (2003) as the attempt to unravel meaning through an interpretative engagement with the transcripts and the identification of themes and clusters within and across cases.

Outcomes

The following outcomes were identified by the study:

Retention

Just under half (20) of the students in the sample were still attending secondary school at the age of 14. Less than a third (13) of students (8 girls and 5 boys) completed secondary education to the age of 16. Componential analysis revealed no discernible relationship between a student's likelihood of staying on in school and individual student attainment levels, schools' experience of admitting and teaching Gypsy Traveller students, the size of the school, or the distance between home and school. The following factors were, however, associated with successful retention in school:

- Having parents who expressed a sustained positive attitude about the value of secondary education and a wish for their children to gain appropriate examination passes that would lead to a 'good job.' Analysis of the parent interviews from the retained group revealed that the majority of parents (10 out of 13) consistently made statements that reflected a high value attached to secondary education

- Having older brothers and sisters who had themselves engaged in education until the age of 16 and who reported positive school experiences. Just over half of the retained students had older siblings that had completed secondary school

- Having high expectations in terms of aspirations, and having these shared by parents

■ Having good interpersonal skills and secure friendship networks that included both Gypsy Traveller and non-Gypsy Traveller peers. Eleven of the thirteen students who were successfully retained in school until the age of 16 were open about their identity, mixed with peers from both groups in and out of school and played an active part in school life, including extra curricular activities (see below)

■ Regular school attendance and participation in a range of extra-curricular activities such as choir, football and drama. There was an apparent link between those students who did not take part in such activity and early drop-out.

Just over half the students who completed their secondary education planned to continue their education beyond 16, and had successfully achieved places at colleges of further education. Three had enrolled on Hairdressing courses, one opted for Beauty Therapy, one for Health and Social Care, one for Sports Studies and the other planned to study Vehicle Maintenance. Of the remaining six, three males planned to work with relatives, one female had found employment in an animal centre and the remaining two females, who had both planned to continue into further education, were reconsidering their options after achieving lower examination results than they had expected.

Drop-out
Over two thirds of the students (31) left the school system at various points during the study:

■ 6 failed to transfer to secondary school

■ 6 dropped out in the first year (age 11-12)

■ 9 dropped out in second year (age 12-13)

■ 3 dropped out in the third year (age 13-14)

■ 6 dropped out in the fourth year (age 14-15)

■ 1 dropped out during the final year (age 16).

This finding highlights the important message that, whether Gypsy Traveller children live in houses or on the roadside, their engagement in secondary education is vulnerable. Factors associated with school drop-out were:

- having parents who expressed negative attitudes about secondary education and a weak affiliation with mainstream culture
- attendance at large, high performing schools
- a history of poor school attendance
- having older brothers and sisters with unhappy experiences in secondary school. Patterns of confrontational or unhappy secondary school experiences tended to be repeated in families
- open and predetermined intentions to leave school early
- incidents of racially motivated conflict and bullying
- gender – twice as many boys (16) dropped out as girls (8).

Boys were proportionately more likely than girls to drop out early and their withdrawal was often preceded by a breakdown in relationships between home and school. In a sense, parents were placing schools on trial and when students were unhappy in school, parents were reluctant to compel them to attend.

Under-achievement

In common with earlier studies (Ofsted 1996, 1999, and 2003), this research identified under-achievement amongst Gypsy Traveller students in both primary and secondary national assessment results. At the end of key stage 3 (age 14), out of 44 children:

- only 20 per cent achieved the expected level or above in English tests, compared with around 70 per cent of students nationally
- 35 per cent per cent achieved expected levels in maths and science tests, compared with around 70 per cent of students nationally.

At the end of key stage 4 (age 16):

- only three students (7%) passed 5 GCSEs (or equivalent) at grade A-C, compared with 61 per cent of students nationally
- ten students (23%) achieved 5 GCSEs (or equivalent) at grade A-G compared with 98 per cent of students nationally.

Attainment levels were also analysed in terms of 'value added' i.e. progress in attainment during secondary school. It was found that only half the students maintained their standards of attainment in English and only four added value to their achievement in maths and science.

Attendance

The teachers described more than three-quarters of the students in the sample as having irregular attendance. Those with the worst attendance also experienced difficulties in social relationships and the majority of poor attenders had left school by the age of 14. The study found that attendance was not always monitored or rigorously followed up by schools and that teachers had low expectations generally about Gypsy Traveller students' attendance. Some schools relied on Gypsy Traveller liaison workers to act as the go-between over issues of attendance, rather than making contact with parents directly and we found a lack of confidence in terms of how far Gypsy Traveller parents could be challenged about their parental responsibilities in this respect. Only two sets of parents had been threatened with prosecution for failing to present their children for school but neither case was heard in court as parents claimed to have made arrangements for home education.

Attempts by some schools to encourage disaffected students to remain in education by offering them part-time or reduced timetables were unsuccessful for the four students in this study offered such an arrangement. All dropped out of school by the age of 14. Scrutiny of attendance records also revealed a high incidence of medical absence in some cases and, although these were authorised, interviews with staff revealed concern about the prevalence and authenticity of such absences, suggesting that they suspected that parents were probably colluding with their children. Official guidance states that if the authenticity of the medical absence is in doubt, schools should contact the School Health Service or the family medical practitioner but no examples of this type of follow-up were reported. The study found that illness-related absence was often linked to episodes of bullying or other social or emotional difficulties, which also placed parents under stress. One student presented with school

25

phobia and others engaged in daily battles with their parents in their attempt to avoid school.

In other cases, attendance problems arose when home-school relationships became particularly strained after a behaviour incident or an imposed sanction that was considered unfair by parents. This was more likely to occur in schools that relied heavily on Gypsy Traveller Education service staff to maintain contact with families.

Reasons for non-attendance are therefore complex and the problem needs to be addressed by analysing the predicament from different perspectives to encourage joint problem solving. Schools and policy makers may be able to use a carrot and stick approach effectively to tackle casual truancy, but this is unlikely to address the underlying psycho-social problems that faced some of the students in this study.

Cultural expectations

When the pupils were aged 11, more than half the parents expected their sons and daughters to follow traditional and cultural gender-based roles in adult life. This expectation included the assumption that their children would leave school early. Fifteen students and their parents correctly predicted at the age of 11 that they would be out of the school system by the age of 14. In the UK, young people are generally expected to continue their engagement in full-time education or training beyond the age of sixteen and raising young people's engagement in education and training has become government policy.

With the loss of the youth labour market and the increase in further and higher education engagement, the period of financial dependency has necessarily been extended and many young people do not achieve financial independence until their mid-twenties. Within Gypsy Traveller communities, these adult markers of marriage, autonomy and financial independence are expected to arrive significantly earlier. But traditional cultural attitudes and expectations are shifting. Over a third of the mothers spoke positively, for example, about the value of a secondary education and wanted their children to enjoy greater opportunities than they themselves had experienced. Whilst a number of the parents articulated high aspirations for their sons and daughters, vocational skills were usually given a higher priority than academic qualifications. The achievement of a functional level of literacy was perceived to be the determining factor of a 'good education' and was commonly associated with being a 'scholar'.

Amongst all parents, the will or desire to keep aspects of the Gypsy Traveller culture alive was evident. The vast majority of the students said they knew and spoke a language at home in addition to English. They described this as Romani, Gaelic or 'Gypsy Traveller language' (Anglo-Romani or Gammon). Interviews also revealed the value placed on the maintenance of Gypsy Traveller customs and traditions regardless of whether families lived in trailers or houses.

Racism

The majority of students (almost 80%) said they were sometimes called racist names or were subjected to bullying in school. This was particularly prevalent during the first weeks and months at a new secondary school and usually took place outside the classroom, during breaks, when moving between lessons or on the journey to and from school. In most cases, this abuse was described as an occasional rather than a regular occurrence, although in a handful of cases, the bullying carried on over several weeks or had continued intermittently over two or three years. As well as direct name-calling there was evidence of more subtle tactics employed by girls who socially excluded Gypsy Traveller peers or who made indirect racist remarks in their hearing. Six students (four boys and two girls) were physically attacked, pushed down stairs and beaten, or had been threatened with offensive weapons. A key issue appeared to be that systems of support and official procedures to address and deal with race-related bullying relied upon children and parents reporting them. Where senior school staff were alerted to racial harassment by the parents of the victims, this was usually seen to be dealt with effectively at the time by the mothers and students concerned.

In almost two-thirds of cases, however, racist bullying or harassment was not reported to teachers. The underlying perception of the students was that institutional racism pervaded the system and prevented fair treatment: 'the other kids just deny it so we don't bother', 'they said it was me and the teachers believed them'. Despite this culture of non-reporting, teachers were usually made aware of conflicts because the students' coping strategies often entailed physical or verbal retaliation. Almost half the pupils had been reprimanded or punished for physical acts that were, according to the students, responses to racist name-calling or bullying. Many Gypsy Traveller parents encouraged their children to settle disputes and deal with provocation by standing up for themselves. As one mother commented: 'How can you tell a Travelling kid that the best man walks away? The best man doesn't walk away ... it's bred in them.' Other coping strategies included avoidance, such as feigned illness linked to absence from school, developing allegiance with the bullies for self protection, and gaining support from older siblings, relatives or Gypsy Traveller friends.

Cultural identity

Typically, the Gypsy Traveller children were very much in the minority at school. Many were the only Gypsy Travellers in their primary school class and this minority status became more marked as students transferred to secondary school. Thirty-two students (84%) transferred to secondary schools with less than five other Traveller students in their year group. There were perceived advantages and disadvantages associated with this minority position. Although students valued social support from Gypsy Traveller peers they were conscious that stereotyped attitudes could disadvantage them at school. Students adopted a range of strategies to cope with their minority status. Four of the girls were found to hide, mask or deny their cultural and ethnic identity at secondary school. Several others said that their siblings, cousins or acquaintances also adopted this tactic known as 'passing', which is said to be used for self-protection in the context of co-existing within a predominantly hostile and prejudiced majority culture (Hancock, 1997). Six other students were guarded about their heritage culture and only disclosed details of their backgrounds gradually once trust had developed with close friends.

When you get talking to people and they ask you where you live, sometimes I tell them and they are OK, sometimes they go off you when they know and sometimes I don't bother telling them about who I really am ... it's better not to.

Where Gypsy Traveller children find themselves straddling two cultural worlds, different and sometimes contradictory expectations from home and school can result in cultural dissonance. Values that are prized in one culture may be rejected in the other and a sense of discord or disharmony can arise when these differences are unexplained or unexpected. Children may find themselves torn between two sets of loyalties, although the evidence from this study suggests that, publicly at least, family loyalties tend to take precedence. For example, parental anxieties meant that some children were not allowed to attend sex education lessons, take part in educational visits involving travel and/or overnight stays or engage in extra curricula activities. These students told the researchers that they understood and were untroubled by these parental constraints, although parents themselves hinted otherwise.

Behaviour

The behaviour of the majority of students was considered by their teachers to be good until the age of 13. Generally students and their parents were accepting of school rules but sanctions imposed sometimes caused conflict, particularly the issuing of detentions. The way in which some Gypsy Traveller students communicated with adults was perceived to be inappropriate by some teachers and could lead to tensions. In a few cases inadequate levels of support for students with special educational needs led to behavioural difficulties.

The students themselves were positive about their relationships with most of their teachers. In several cases, the problem behaviour was contextual rather than generic, suggesting that the relationship with particular individual teachers was a key factor. Some students, for example, had very mixed progress reports, with glowing comments interspersed with extremely negative appraisals of their behaviour. More than a third of the students said they believed that certain teachers harboured and conveyed racist attitudes towards them. A number of the students, mainly boys, were perceived to react inappropriately when reprimanded and agitated their teachers by always having the last word. There was a perception amongst some teachers that Gypsy Traveller children had more freedom at home and were treated more as adults, so found it difficult to accept authority at school. Interviews revealed some truth in this assumption, particularly in relation to domestic and life skills, but also revealed highly protective parenting styles and a sheltered upbringing.

The study also found a high level of exclusion. A quarter of the students (nine boys and three girls) had been excluded from school at least once, usually for acts of physical aggression towards peers or verbal abuse towards staff. As already suggested, many parents and students felt that Gypsy Travellers were excluded for retaliating towards other students' racist behaviour.

Conclusions

The successful retention of Gypsy Traveller students in secondary education is not simply a matter of access and continuity. As this study clearly illustrates, settled or largely sedentary Gypsy Traveller children are highly unlikely to complete their statutory period of secondary education and we need to consider a wider range of variables (other than mobility) in order to understand why so many Traveller pupils have irregular attendance and leave school early.

In our attempt to disentangle and identify the causes of secondary retention problems, we have reached a view that too much emphasis on cultural expectations can lead to a theory of cultural pathology in which other related factors may be insufficiently considered. Parental and community attitudes that apparently challenge or reject mainstream educational values may be borne out of a genuine and deep-seated mistrust of the settled community and fears for childrens' physical and emotional well being. Not only do many Gypsy Traveller students in school have to deal with cultural dissonance but most encounter racism and social or cultural alienation. All these influences affect the young person's development of identity and self-concept. Fundamentally, socio-psychocultural factors will shape a student's identity as a learner and will influence their educational experiences. Individuals who feel isolated, socially and culturally, are unlikely to reach their full potential in such an environment.

Notes

1 The term Gypsy Traveller is used throughout and encompasses English Gypsy Travellers and children of Irish Traveller heritage. Other Travellers such as occupational, and Fairground and Circus Showmen were not included in this study.

2 Most LAs (local authorities) have dedicated Traveller Education Services usually made up of peripatetic teachers, learning support assistants and field-workers who work in schools and the community to promote mainstream education and to increase the attendance and attainment of Gypsy Traveller students at school

3

The irresistible attraction of Information and Communication Technology: experiences of trainee teachers from minority ethnic backgrounds

Ghazala Bhatti

Senior Lecturer at the School of Education,
University of Southampton, England

Teachers have a profound effect on children's learning. The absence of teachers in mainstream classrooms who represent a rich diversity of ethnicities sends out a powerful message to all our children. Recruiting competent Black and South Asian teachers would help all children to identify with school and, in the long run, contribute to society. This issue has implications for social justice, not just in Britain but in the whole of Europe.

The idea of social justice as re-distributive justice facilitates connecting theory and practice. It values agency and challenges stagnation and inaction (Young, 1990; Fraser, 1997; Gerwirtz, 1998; Griffths, 2003). 'Equality of opportunity' and 'equality of outcome' sound hollow unless a society actively seeks to create circumstances in which all communities feel accepted and are able to make a positive contribution. Teaching in schools offers a practical opportunity for transforming the lives of teachers and students. It has long been known that aspiring teachers from minority ethnic backgrounds face more problems than their majority ethnic colleagues (Osler, 1997; Hoodless, 2004; Basit *et al*, 2006). Powney *et al* (2003) documented the experiences of 2158 teachers. They reported persistent discrimination when it came to issues of race, age and gender.

Researchers have identified the processes by which inequality is reproduced in educational establishments (Mac an Ghaill, 1988; Sleeter, 1993; Osler, 1994; Gillborn and Youdell, 1999). Positive role models can challenge dis-enfranchisement among under-achieving teenagers, for instance boys from African Caribbean, Pakistani and Bangladeshi backgrounds (Bhatti, 1999; Gordon, 2000; Cork, 2005). The cost of leaving this human resource under-developed in social, political and economic terms is enormous.

Taking a university in England as an example, this chapter looks at a post-graduate programme which continues to attract and retain trainee teachers from minority ethnic and less privileged backgrounds. Their involvement with secondary schools provides an opportunity to interact with pupils who are close to school leaving age; some of them never return to formal education. So this PGCE (Post Graduate Certificate in Education) in ICT (Information and Communications Technology) has relevance for other teacher training courses in England and other European countries.

As recipients of the British schooling system and as future teachers, research participants reflected on thought provoking issues which are challenging for teachers, schools and training institutions. Current discussions about widening participation involve British universities, which are held accountable for admitting non-traditional participants from lower socio-economic groups and people from minority ethnic backgrounds (Reay, 1997; Bhatti, 2001, 2003). This raises questions. Do teacher training programmes in universities have 'under-subscribed' and 'over-subscribed' subjects where they compete to attract and retain trainee teachers? If so, which areas are most attractive? Do subjects which 'successfully' recruit future teachers from under-represented backgrounds have anything to teach us?

The study

This study, conducted between 2003 and 2004, is based on several long ethnographic interviews collected at the beginning and end of a PGCE. Looking at widening participation in general, and the participation of minority ethnic students in particular, it was clear that the PGCE programme which was, and continues to be, most popular is ICT. Almost half its intake in a typical year is from people from diverse backgrounds who are highly motivated and interested in teaching, whereas other subjects rarely attract and retain similar students.

It was interesting to discover why members from minority ethnic communities chose ICT rather than Science, History, English or Maths. As the research progressed, many intertwined reasons came to light. Some were predictable, while others revealed unsolicited information relating some disturbing findings which reflect broader social issues facing secondary school teachers.

All 29 trainee teachers were invited, but the ten who were most interested in taking part in the research were three women and seven men, from the following ethnic and religious groups: African Caribbean (Seventh Day Adventist), Iraqi (Muslim), Indian (Sikh and Hindu), Irish (Catholic) and Pakistani (Muslim). Most, but not all were hetro-sexual. The average age was 28 years. For the purposes of confidentiality, the themes which emerged are reported rather than presenting individual case studies which might identify participants. After PGCE everyone secured a teaching post in a school of their choice. All fit into the profile of those who use 'instrumentalism' successfully (Bhatti, 2003). However, not all have found the experience unproblematic.

These are intelligent, articulate, confident people, who are aware of possible mis-representation. Five asked if I had ever written anything about people from their ethnic backgrounds. If this research were to be published, would they be mentioned by name? Two read some of my publications before agreeing to participate. This level of probing and accountability demonstrates a growing awareness about research-based evidence among some trainee teachers in Britain. What follows takes account of a need to be very candid and wholly anonymous. The tape-recorded interviews were semi-structured and open-ended. Participants could at any time withdraw or add to information by phone, e-mail, a meeting, or could refuse to continue. These are the themes that emerged.

Memories of school

Each participant is the first in their family to graduate. All had attended secondary schools and obtained first degrees in Britain. Not everyone went on to study PGCE immediately. They came from different careers related to ICT. Some had other interests (hobbies/ paid/voluntary work) such as community and youth work, architecture and music. Others had backgrounds in philosophy, art, disc-jockeying, catering and lightweight boxing.

They related varied experiences of schooling, not all of them positive. One man mentioned a teacher from his own ethnic background 'but she taught remedial kids and was not respected'. This tallies with previous research findings (Bhatti, 1999). None knew a senior teacher they could 'relate to as one of our kind, to put it bluntly!' There was a Chemistry teacher 'from India I think ...she was a lab technician'. Research indicates that until recently teachers who qualified overseas were considered unworthy of the same salary scales as locally trained teachers. Until the early 1990s many were not employed as mainstream teachers. Some worked as Section 11 teachers, others as teacher assistants (McEachron and Bhatti, 2005).

'Bad company' and 'losing my way totally in my teenage [years]' were mentioned, as were 'getting lost in a college of further education, not knowing it was for losers', and of 'racial bullying when teachers didn't know what to do'. Many dealt with racism on their own and saw it as a 'fact of life'. Those with older siblings found life easier. Others related stories of public praise by teachers for the benefit of 'otherwise dumpy class fellows from similar backgrounds... so, so embarrassing!'

Some individual teachers in secondary schools were inspirational. It was this experience which was partly responsible for their considering teaching as a profession. *Not one* of those who were spoken about spontaneously and warmly were ICT teachers, but then ICT was not taught when they were at school themselves.

36

Role models

The male participants were explicit about their positive male role models:

> My father has worked very hard in his life. He tried to give us what he didn't have himself, so you kind of felt bad to let him down.

> My Dad kept us from kids who dossed around. He said you are seen as 'a black boy' at school and don't... forget it. You'll be ignored by teachers if you hang around with the baddies and no-gooders.' So we tried not to be seen with some kinds of children...in secondary school we had to come home by a certain time... Otherwise there was hell!

> My father who worked in a factory retired after...hard work. He's a ...honest, decent, religious man. He is my role model, my inspiration, not my school teachers, not my professors... he taught me the real meaning of human worth and dignity.

For other views on this issue see Sewell (1997) and Cork (2005).

Neither the men nor the women mentioned their mothers in similar vein, even though many had been brought up by working mothers, and in three cases single mothers. This is noteworthy, particularly in the case of women who chose not to mention either parent. This might be because women's work in the home was taken for granted in their families.

Why teach?

Teaching was not always the first choice; some moved to teaching for job security. This may be a common factor for some mature PGCE students. Opting for teaching caused participants to adopt a new identity. The most striking example was a Hindu man who re-signed from a multinational firm in the USA. He decided to return to 'good old England 'after the 'paranoia following 9/11'. He took pains to point out that he is not Muslim but that because 'all Indian look-ing people were under fire', he had to resign. Working in the USA was 'OK until the watershed when everything changed' and all 'foreigners were seen with loathing and suspicion'. Teaching was a useful career while he was settling in England again with a young family, even though it meant considerable loss of earnings for him and his wife. Ironically, in 2004 I had asked him half-jokingly what he would do if something similar happened in England, and he had replied 'Europe is a wiser, reasonable place. Can it happen here?.. if it does? We will handle it without paranoia!'

Many participants wanted the 'satisfaction of having a direct, positive influence on the younger generation' (also see Jones *et al*, 1997). One had current experience of youth work with African Caribbean boys from his local church. A Pakistani man involved in raising the aspirations of Pakistani boys from his local mosque, spoke with dismay about children's 'under-achievement and their parents' shocking ignorance and illiteracy'. None of the women spoke of emotive engagement with community based pre-occupations.

Religion as a barrier or a motive for teaching?
Four participants from Catholic, Muslim and Sikh backgrounds mentioned the influence of religion in their communities.

Women who wear the *hijab* face particular barriers, which one woman described as 'unspoken but very real'. The coverage of the issue in the French media surfaced at a time when one woman wearing a *hijab* entered an all white suburban school. Some white middle class teachers were unable to comprehend that 'I can be interested in ICT... !' and that 'the *hijab* does not mean I am brain dead!' They explained their preservation of the self (Woods, 1983) and their coping strategies in these terms:

> I don't think about how I am received. I just go in and pretend there is nothing different about me at all.

> They were a little shocked. They had a negative impression of me, thinking that I won't last very long, but I did.

There was a sense of exhilaration when those impressions were proved wrong. There was also a quiet, self-generated pressure to perform well without expecting help from school.

Men who had beards, whether Sikh and Muslim, were seen as 'fundamentalist weirdo' by white teachers in secondary schools.

One participant smiled about it, saying:

> It is in the look I get, but so what? I am here to teach and once I start doing that, things are bound to fall into place. I like working with children, all children. What's my beard got to do with ICT?

This man had experience in industry and he did not let his mentor's 'unprofessional behaviour' get in the way of his development. Alongside ICT, he taught religious education. His job references were written by the teacher who had invited him to contribute to religious education, rather than his ICT teacher and mentor.

> I spoke of Malcolm X and his spiritual journey to Mecca. The children were very open minded, very interested! I mean white children, all children.

He tried to universalise the notion of pilgrimage, of travelling to a place to 'find oneself', and all the children in Year Seven were interested in Malcolm X as an iconic figure. He felt 'under-utilised'. However, that gave him time to prepare good lessons for the children he was teaching, and he spoke about them with warmth and affection. He did not perceive his mentor's behaviour as racist – the mentor did not reply to e-mails and would not support the trainee teacher in class. He dismissed the mentor's behaviour as 'discourteous and unprofessional'. I later discovered, through conversation with his university tutor, that the mentor did not feel he had been unsupportive. When the student got upset and walked out of a meeting with his mentor, it was put down to a 'personality clash'. An African Caribbean student got on well with the same mentor.

The experience for Catholic teachers surviving secular schools was expressed as follows: 'the best thing to do... was to go underground and have a professional not a religious identity,' 'but then there is the Irish accent that gives it all away!' Ireland had 'equipped people to accept religion as a fact of life [England] is different.' The exploitation of ordinary people in Northern Ireland in the name of religion was raised and this participant remarked how getting involved in sport made 'all male teachers popular with all kinds of kids'. Sport was used as a coping strategy and as a form of continuing with 'life as it was before I decided to become a teacher'. I was told that religion was 'fore-grounded in Ireland and back-grounded in England'. The challenge of teaching ICT in secular schools was welcomed, though England was experienced as a little strange and a 'deep culture shock' because of the lack of religious observance.

Experiences of exclusion

Two men, a Sikh and a Muslim mentioned 'cliques' among students on the PGCE course based on social class, gender and ethnicity. Married women from white middle class backgrounds who were 'doing PGCE as an additional source of income' were perceived as 'socially inaccessible'. They would not socialise with non-white PGCE students. It was not possible to verify this data across the whole cohort, as this was revealed right at the end of the year when everyone was about to leave. There was discussion about subject specific knowledge and the ways in which participants made sense of their experiences, which in terms of professional development can be seen as 'communities of practice' (Wenger, 1998).

Quality of learning

Most participants complained about the amount of preparation, of nervous moments when things 'looked like they were going to take more than two hours ... every night after whole days of thinking and teaching'. At the end of PGCE a feeling of achievement coincided with self-affirmation and buoyancy. Two participants wanted to pursue part-time studies and enrolled on a Masters Degree in Inclusive Education in their first year of teaching. Many underestimated the 'paper work that goes to make up the life of a teacher in England'. They were happy with most elements of training, though three mentioned that there was insufficient discussion of 'equal opportunities and things like that'.

> We are supposed to be living side by side with different cultures, but we don't discuss issues which make up British society – is it indifference, tolerance or fear of rocking the (ethnic) boat?'

Another participant suggested

> I suppose they (real issues) have nothing to do directly with ICT, so we talk about safe and stupid things like the weather and football. Very intellectual...

Some schools were praised for supportive mentors, others were 'backward'. PGCE students spoke of 'really hitting it off with the head of the department who wants me to consider working permanently at my placement school'. Legal issues were mentioned about 'dodgy' situations where trainee teachers were left alone in a class to manage challenging behaviour from pupils, such as bullying and even attempted self-harm.

Intellectual journey

For four students this was a life changing experience, forcing them to think deeply about social issues. One participant could not wait to read the Sunday newspaper 'without that creeping guilt for not pre-paring perfect lessons, for always being on trial, not doing enough work', for another 'life was on hold – sort of on 'pause' button – and waiting to be picked up where I left it'. Two students played sport, which took their minds off teaching. One said he would start writing a diary of his experiences as he faces 'the world's future hope as a teacher of young minds'. Something in school was so moving that 'it has made a writer of me!' Among authors read for pleasure during the demanding year, were mentioned: Giddens, Vikram Seth, Asimov and 'that author of *The Selfish Gene*. The idea of ICT seen as a non-creative subject was challenged and heatedly refuted.

> Most people probably think I am a very boring person... can that be? I have to enter the minds of young people and engage with the younger generation. ICT is 'cool' if you can use the white board interactively, surely?

Many participants enjoyed using modern technology as a tool for learning, amusement and 'for real pure fun in class'.

For the majority of the participants a year at university caused apprehension at the beginning and achievement at the end, not so much for technical skills, but for the 'sheer staying power'. This meant survival among children and teachers in schools and peers at university. The main challenge on the PGCE course was seen by every one as 'much more social than technical or intellectual'.

'Is it the subject or am I just any teacher?' one participant asked aloud

> I am a teacher who happens to teach ICT, but I am a teacher in the first instance.

41

Another point raised often was 'Which subjects teach a universal, global text? – ICT and music!'

Vocation and survival

Except in the case of the two religious (Catholic and Muslim) people, most participants thought learning to teach was all about self-discovery and self-knowledge, that it pointed the way to 'survival with respect ' and to 'a decent standard of living', which might become a life time commitment.

> It all depends on how schools treat me. They say once you are into... mid-thirties you get stuck and are not promoted as an Asian person, let's see, I haven't got there yet!

> It is a job as jobs go! If I manage to find a welcoming school, I may stay...

> It is a boring question... knuckling down and sticking it out. Not letting petty things get to you...there will be politics. But then all jobs have politics when it comes to promotions and salaries... Why just blame teaching?

It meant a lot to these PGCE students when they made it to the end of the year.

Family matters

Three of the men with young children were keen to get home to relieve their wives of childcare. Socialising depended on the travelling distance between home and university, and between home and school. In one case, the wife could work only after the husband had returned home. In another case, two primary school aged children were being home-schooled by the parents, both British graduates, and this placed a particular demand on spare time for other activities, including research interviews.

Some of the Muslim trainee teachers expressed their resistance to Muslim schools. Others felt they would not send their own children to any state school and would home school them instead:

> I would not like to have gone to a Muslim school for Muslim girls. My life would have been... limited. I have a Palestinian friend who is studying in London University... went to a Muslim girls school

> and found university very difficult. She felt... lost. (24 year old Iraqi woman. She wears a *hijab* and is a practising Muslim.)

> I went through a strange system. I am learning to teach and then I will educate my own children at home. My wife has a degree in the sciences. She is at home looking after our two young children. She prefers to do that, as do many English (white) professional women with young children. It is her choice. It is not a 'Muslim thing'. No, I don't want my children to be exposed to oppression in British schools! We will educate them at home. (35 year old Pakistani man)

These are just two views from the field. They might not be typical of Muslim trainee teachers, but they are significant because they capture the dichotomy about educational futures and the possible educational trajectories for these trainees' children and the next generation.

Fatherhood and ICT

It was easier to combine teaching responsibilities with fatherhood.

> Everything I learn at school will help me to understand my own kid when he starts school. My father had no idea what I faced when I went to school.

> Teachers know more about children than many other people in society! It will help me become a better parent. I will find out about the good schools...

None of the women mentioned motherhood, perhaps because none of them were mothers. They talked exclusively about their professional identities and ambitions, whereas men discussed broader issues and with greater ease and humour. It may be that men welcomed the opportunity to discuss such topics in confidence.

The pain of rejection

Some participants had faced redundancies and resignations. They saw teaching as different:

> If worst came to worst I can do temporary supply teaching.

> At least I will not starve! If I force myself go to tough and rough schools in London, there will be many jobs...

Another participant said

I can't bear to think about it, but I have braced myself. Who knows how it will feel if I don't get a teaching job in the city I want to work in?

The fear of failing kept some focused on their studies. One participant had suffered from mental illness and was terrified of becoming unemployed as his cousins had been.

It (rejection) has happened before- only it has been in holiday jobs when it didn't matter- now it damn well will!

In the event every single person on the programme found employment. There is a continuing demand for teachers in ICT and at least some of the fear was unfounded.

Why ICT?

ICT gave teachers more transferable skills in Britain today than other subjects. It had a ' universal appeal' and 'international job opportunities:

I mean who in their right mind will teach British or Roman History as an Indian man? a – would you get a decent job, b – is that a field where you could excel even if you wanted to? You will be blocked straightaway!

Teaching English to English kids being a black man is bit of a joke! I think it is better to write poetry (referring to Benjamin Zephaniah) than to pretend to love [Jane] Austen and all that!

I like the fun you can have with computers and children, which you just can't have smelling lovely chemicals in a Chemistry lab... nothing against Chemistry. It is just not my thing ... or Biology.

There were few opportunities for these students to interact with PGCE students studying other subjects.

Feeling valued in society and creating cohesion within the group

Most participants felt that society did not value teachers enough, but their immediate family members did. Moral support came from people who were supportive of the individuals and the teaching profession, such as a girlfriend (1) parents (4) fiancée (1) wife (3). The group did not socialise as a whole after lectures, unless there was an

44

organised party at the university. There were two main reasons for this. The first was that teaching placements did not occur in the same geographical location, except where a school was willing to accept two students. The other was that not everyone lived on campus, and therefore could not meet in the evenings or at the end of the day. Consequently a PGCE which is open to mature students is experienced in a different way from PGCE which mainly recruits newly qualified graduates.

Children and the secret lives of trainee teachers

What children think about their teachers matters to them (Bhatti 2004), and this in turn affects their teaching. For trainee teachers it also affects their coping strategies inside and outside the classroom.

> It is boy thing!' I am a positive role model for the boys, and I know it. Sad isn't it? But it really really helps to be good at football.

This trainee discovered to his horror that older schoolgirls found him attractive. He was terrified and did not discuss it with other teachers. Instead spent all his break times with the boys on the playing field.

> I mean I don't want any trouble. PGCE is enough trouble as it is!

He thought the matter was a taboo subject at school and that neither the university nor the school equipped him to deal with it.

Other participants felt that the children were far too curious for their own good.

> It is like this, I want to be seen as teacher and that is all. I draw a line.

A Sikh participant spoke about how children tried to find out about his religion. 'I went out of my way *not* to tell them. I did not want things... to get in the way of my teaching or their perception of me.' He told me he was 'adopted' by Muslim boys who stayed on 'just to have a little chat about life, where I lived, did I play cricket'.

One participant mentioned fear, sleepless nights and anxieties over what would happen if the children from the placement school found out

say, wandering around in the shopping centre, that my partner is
the same sex as me!

This experience is not unique for teachers (see Sullivan, 1993).
Schools are among many of the institutions where hetero-sexual
identities are considered to be the norm.

Racism

Issues of racism were interwoven in the answers to other questions
rather than pulled out specially for comment. Almost all the participants said that contrary to their expectation and to what they read
in the media about 'laddish behaviour and teenage thugs', the children were kind, open-minded and tolerant, provided that lessons
were well planned and delivered competently. Children were
genuinely interested in trainee teachers. This optimistic outlook was
true of white middle class children in village schools and the diverse
populations of inner city schools. Some dismay was expressed at
perceived intolerance from adults in these same schools, including
teachers, porters and cleaners.

One student had experienced racism in the university but he was
not prepared to elaborate. Almost all others mentioned experiences...

> out there in the community over the years...

> It is a sad fact of life, you can't let it get you down, can you?

They were less concerned about social racism than about professional or 'institutional' racism (Macpherson, 1999), particularly
when they thought it might affect their prospects for promotion.

Conclusion

The research reported here is a glimpse behind the scenes. It reveals
the reflections and experiences of an interesting and accomplished
group of professionals who will surely enrich the lives of their students and colleagues. Although they belong to communities of practice where subject specific issues and competent teaching were discussed, they were profoundly silent about other important issues
which were revealed during the research. They displayed optimism,
humour, determination, perseverance and a will to succeed. They

thought they would become good role models if the schools where they work are mature enough, willing and able enough to work with them in positive ways. Their contribution to mostly English schools goes beyond their subject specialism.

As they gain in confidence, these future teachers will, by their very presence in classrooms, in playgrounds, in staff rooms, challenge racisms, sexism and other kinds of inequalities. Their future contribution to enhancing the quality of teaching in schools will, it is hoped, add a new dimension to growing evidence of social justice in action within education. If ICT is an area which has high status in schools, the future direction for teacher training seems optimistic – at least for future teachers from minority ethnic backgrounds who choose this particular field.

The research found a notable silence about issues which go beyond teaching students competence in their subjects. If we acknowledge the educational and social benefits which derive from the re-generation of communities which have been caught up in a cyclical experience of disempowerment, mistrust and under-development, then there is really no argument against an active representation from all communities on the teaching body. Those who participated willingly in this research might by their example encourage more young people to join the teaching profession. What is reported about England may be equally true of many other countries in Europe.

Section II
Intercultural challenges

4

Learning to be in public spaces: in from the margins with dancers, sculptors, painters and musicians

Morwenna Griffiths

Professor of Classroom Learning at the Moray House
School of Education, Edinburgh University, Scotland

*with Judy Berry, Anne Holt, John Naylor
and Philippa Weekes*

of Nottingham University, England

Introduction

This chapter explores one way in which the arts can work for social justice in schools. It argues that arts-based work in school has helped disadvantaged or disaffected children to engage in arts-based and other activities, and to grow in the exercise of voice and agency as they did so. The artists may include dancers, filmmakers, installation artists, landscape artists, sculptors, musicians, painters, potters, storytellers and others.

The account is compiled by a university-based researcher working in partnership with teacher-researchers. It evolved during a research project developing a model for learning in the arts. The project related to work in Creative Partnerships, a national government initiative to encourage creativity and learning (and we are grateful to Creative Partnerships Nottingham for providing the funding that enabled this research) The authors of the chapter are as follows. Judy Berry is the head of Rufford Infant (ages 3-7), where Anne Holt is a teacher. John Naylor teaches in Shepherd, a special school for children of all ages with profound learning difficulties. Philippa Weekes is the deputy head of Seagrave Primary (ages 3-11). All the schools are in Nottingham. Each school carried out an action research project. Morwenna Griffiths is a university professor who acted as a critical friend and adviser for these school-based projects, in a partnership in which each person contributed their particular skills and knowledge. The chapter draws on research reports by John and Philippa and on a leaflet produced with Rufford School at the end of the project.

The chapter contributes to a small but growing educational literature on the role of the arts in education for social justice and inclusion. The arts have been seen as a way of acknowledging, respecting and working with the diversity of artistic expression in society. They are seen as helping students see the relevance to their own lives of work in schools while at the same time increasing their understanding of the cultural heritage of others. Maxine Greene's work in North America on the role of the arts in education was influential. She discusses the arts in relation to what she terms the social imagination. She argues that making poetic use of imagination enables us 'to be in some manner a participant in artists' worlds reaching far back and ahead in time' (Greene, 1995:4). So she connects the arts to 'becoming wide-awake to the world' as well to 'discovering cultural diversity [and] to making community' (Greene, 1995:4). She argues further that it is this poetic use of imagination that can enable students to conceive of and work towards social justice:

> We also have our social imagination: the capacity to invent visions of what should be and what might be in our deficient society, on the streets where we live, in our schools. (Greene, 1995:5)

Methodology

Our methodology is rooted in two modes of inquiry: philosophical investigation and action research. The abstractions of the former are put into iterative interaction with the specificities of the latter. The philosophical issue is the connection between individual voice and the space in which individual voices can come together in collective action. The action research is school-based and teacher-led, a methodology described by Griffiths (2003) as practical philosophy. It is self-consciously and explicitly distinct from forms of philosophy which distance themselves from empirical concerns. Equally, it is self-consciously and explicitly distinct from applied philosophy. In applied philosophy, abstractions are applied to practical contexts. In contrast, practical philosophy is 'a kind of philosophy that is interested in the empirical world as a way of grounding its conclusions in interaction between thinking and acting' (Griffiths, 2003:21).

Thus there is continuing attention is paid to practicalities and specificities while theorising, and to careful, rigorous theorising and reflection while carrying out practice. Philosophy of this sort requires a kind of conversation, an interaction, between the two modes of understanding. So it is a philosophy as, with and for... rather than philosophy about or applied; a kind of philosophy that acknowledges its own roots in the communities from which it sprang, and which then speaks with – at least – that community. It is no accident that this methodology is appropriate for social justice research. It is part of a movement from, in Michael Oakeshott's (1962) famous phrase, the 'conversation of mankind' to something more inclusive. It is inclusive of women. It acknowledges that mankind, like womankind, includes groups of people and kinds of conversation which are rarely heard in philosophical circles. It is also inclusive of all kinds of conversation and all kinds of people. In this chapter, the conversation includes teachers as well as academics and, to some extent, young people too.

An obvious difficulty for practical philosophy is finding some common language so that conversation can take place. Philosophical argument is typically conducted in such abstract terms that to take part requires participants to be articulate in these terms. Typically, such participants are highly educated and from a narrow social group. They tend, to use the term introduced by Jean-François Lyotard (1979), to generate 'grand narratives'. At the same time, this group is unlikely to be articulate in the forms of language used for practical understanding. Lyotard is helpful here. He describes society as operating with a heterogeneity of language games which are incommensurable (1979:xxiv). Elsewhere Lyotard terms these language games as 'petits recits' – little stories (Lyotard, 1989). These little stories belong to different forms of discourse which are likely to be incommensurable with each other. However, they can be brought into some kind of communicative interaction with each other even when the marginalised group is unable to fully articulate their experience of reality (Lyotard, 1989; Palermo, 2003) and the dominant one lacks the experiences of the marginalised. Lyotard describes this in terms of a 'differend', a fundamental dispute between language games, which can be brought into linkage, but with no expectation of a final resolution or consensus.

In this chapter, action research is used as a way of linking the conversations in schools with the conversations of philosophers. Action research can be understood as one form of representing little stories; and meta-reflection on individual action research projects can be one way of bringing grand narratives and little stories into conversation with each other. Therefore the methodology of this chapter is an example of practical philosophy, in that it puts abstract theory and little stories – specific, significant narratives of practice – in conversation with each other.

The themes in the three schools featured in this article are as follows: 'Fertile Ground' (Shepherd); 'Children on the Edge' (Seagrave Primary); and 'Children's Voices and Choices' (Rufford Infant). The themes defined by the schools were arrived at independently of each other. But once articulated, they were seen to be interrelated. Taken together they were relevant to the issue of how young people can learn to exercise voice and autonomy, individually and collectively.

The philosophical issue: public spaces and social justice
The idea of public space is central to political philosophy. It is only by establishing a public space that individuals can participate in collective actions and decisions. For collective action to get started, for voice to be exercised, there needs to be a public space in which people can come together. The term public space, as used here, is narrower than as used in ordinary language. It must be a space in which people can interact socially in a joint enterprise, so although

it need not be a physical location it must be a place where people can enter discussion with everybody else there. Thus a shopping mall is not a public space in this sense, but some e-mail lists may be. A cinema is not a public space. A political demonstration such as a march is unlikely to be a public space in this sense, but it could become one. Consider the difference between anti-globalisation demonstrations and the World Social Forum. Only the latter is a public space.

Political philosophy often describes public space in terms of the forum or the agora: a place which is public to everybody. However, this conception is of limited use to marginalised groups who will be excluded from or, at best, ignored in such spaces, and who may even find them dangerous. It is more useful to draw on the idea of Hannah Arendt (1958) that what draws people into collective action are their 'specific, objective, worldly interests' (p182). She goes on to argue that this 'physical, worldly in-between' (p182) is:

> overgrown with an altogether different in-between which consists of deeds and words and owes its origin exclusively to men's acting and speaking directly to one another.... This in-between is no less real than the world of things we visibly have in common. We call this reality the 'web' of human relationships, indicating by the metaphor its somewhat intangible quality. (p183)

This web of relationships is what creates a public space, a space in which collective action is possible. This kind of action is only possible for those who 'know how to enlist the help, the co-acting of [their] fellow men' (p189). It is a public space because the web of relation is between members of the community. It is not the same as the intimate relations between family and friends. It is public in that people are brought together as members of the community by a 'worldly in between'. It is not, however, open to everyone else.

But how do people learn to enter and participate in public-political spaces? When we began this research none of us realised this was an issue. We were not alone in this. Even Hannah Arendt, with all her acute perception about public space, seemed to analyse this issue in purely personal, individual terms. In her discussion of how to facilitate a form of government which fully allowed for the creativity and imagination of each generation to be expressed, she remarks that only some people have 'authentically political talents' (Arendt, 1963:278). Yet it is a commonplace of everyday political life that the people who make use of public spaces are disproportionately the dominant social groups, such as the males of the articulate middle classes. Such effects can be seen in school councils as well as in parent groups or governing bodies. This cannot be simply a matter of inborn inclination and preference. The partipators must have learned how to be and act in public spaces. It was only as a result of participating in the action research reported in this chapter, and alerted by an argument by Jon Nixon (see Griffiths, 2003), that Morwenna came to see the significance of learning the beginnings of the exercise of voice and agency within a public space. At the same time, the action researchers were developing their practical understanding of how children in their schools could participate more fully in school.

The action research (1) Fertile Ground

Shepherd is a special school for pupils of all ages with severe and profound learning difficulties. The school has a long tradition of excellent work in the arts. It might be expected that the Creative Partnerships scheme had little new to offer such a school. It would not have been surprising if involvement in the scheme had simply meant doing more of the same, only better resourced. But John noticed that the school's involvement with Creative Partnerships was taking the excellent work even further and opening up new possibilities. Accordingly, his theme for the action research was: 'The school as fertile ground: How the ethos of a school enables everyone in it to benefit from the presence of artists in class.'

To begin with, evidence was provided by John's reflective diary. As the theme of Fertile Ground emerged, he decided that the mode of reflecting and reporting should match the content. Together with a video maker and some of the pupils, he created a video showing the impact of the partnership work on the school. The work was taken further by examining on-going work with the Theatre of Possibilities, a creative installation involving pupils with profound and multiple learning difficulties. Video was especially appropriate here because

56

these students tend not to access text and do not use writing. Some students use a few single words but most communication is through bodily gesture and some sign language. Inquiry centred on how the process worked, as Creative Partnerships artists extended it, and how this process was dependent on the ethos of the school, and also productive of it. Again, this has been evidenced in a reflective journal and on video.

After a few months it became apparent that the school was finding it easy to cooperate with the Creative Partnerships development worker attached to the school, and the creative practitioners she introduced to it. Projects were abounding and students and staff reported satisfaction and enjoyment in their involvement. Informally comparing themselves to other schools across all age phases throughout the city, they seemed not to be encountering the teething problems reported by other schools working with Creative Partnerships development workers. Shepherd School was negotiating teacher-instigated, pupil-centred, arts-based, creative learning opportunities led by creative practitioners. The school seemed to be successful in terms of the number of fulfilled projects compared to the number planned.

The inquiry suggested how the ethos of the school enables everyone in it to benefit from the presence of artists in class – why it is fertile ground. Notes from John's research log offer the following observations:

> Special schools are used to working in small teams, usually a teacher with a learning support assistant and a care assistant. It is essential that members of these teaching and learning teams *regardless of status* can offer their ideas and observations. The arrival and inclusion of a Creative Partnerships Development Worker adds to the creative dynamic. It is not unusual to be working as a team member, where learners are routinely included in creative activity: the apprenticeship model is exemplified.

An ethos of mutual respect in the public spaces of the school means that different people work together, rather than working as individuals. This way of working respects the different roles of the participants. Students, parents, teachers, dinner nannies, visiting artists and support staff: all have different roles. On the other hand none of these individuals is confined to a narrow interpretation of their role. On the contrary, the ethos encourages everyone to learn from one another as they work together. Evidence collected on video shows some powerful examples of this. Some of what the video revealed prompted a reflection in John's research log:

> Come into the Theatre of Possibilities; walk through the door into the empty darkened stage area. The educational performance is about to start. By analogy we have actors, stage and technical crew, a director with a number of producers. But we have no script. Losing our analogy we have students, learning support assistants, ICT technician, a teacher in charge and we are all a staff of enablers.

The action research (2) Children on the Edge

Seagrave is a large primary and nursery school. Philippa Weekes is the deputy head. Her theme for the action research was: 'Children on the edge: How the arts reach those children who otherwise exclude themselves from class activities for any reason'.

The project was a collaborative one. Philippa encouraged interested members of staff to join her in keeping reflective diaries of the impact of dancers, landscape artists and other creative practitioners on teaching and learning in the school. In the end, five teachers kept diaries. Fortunately, the teachers who had volunteered included representatives from the range of ages in the school, from the Foundation Stage to Year 6, i.e. children aged from 3 to 11. The theme of Children on the Edge emerged after about six months, as the second cycle of the action research. The staff realised that the arts programme appeared to involve the children in the school who otherwise exclude themselves from class activities, because of shyness, behavioural difficulties, disabilities or social difficulties. The team of researchers agreed that they should each focus closely on one or two children on the edge in their classes. As the research progressed, interviews were carried out with children, teachers, parents and artists.

The evidence demonstrates that such children had not only been able to start joining in during creative sessions but had also been slowly joining in other lessons too. For instance, here is Philippa in conversation with a dancer who had done a good deal of work in the school:

> Philippa   And K, you may remember or not, she wouldn't say 'Boo' to a goose and then because you had done that dance she came out of herself and started to talk to people ... Because my sort of thinking research-wise is [your effect on] all those children that are on the edge because of their behaviour, on the edge because of exclusion, or on the edge because they are so quiet they don't say anything, or on the edge because they don't join in. Like you have all those Year 5s: they wouldn't join in at all at the beginning of the term. Five of them refused to do it.

Other teachers had similar comments:

> It allowed quiet children to shine – It's given a boost of confidence, particularly to less academic children or children who do not feel they are a popular member of the class. (Teacher Year 5)

> The confidence boost to N [following a dance performance in a theatre] was astounding and it spilled into other aspects of school life and social skills. (Headteacher)

> Over the year working with Creative Partnerships, H [in Year 5] has become more in control of his own anger, his own emotions. He can now feel for and understand others better. He has matured with the help of expression in a creative manner. (Headteacher)

Children who had seemed to feel that they had no place in a public space – whether because they were shy, lacked confidence, or were disaffected – were able to join in as they wanted to, finding new possibilities of exercising agency. Similarly, it seemed that expressions of feeling which had previously been deemed unacceptable in public were now possible:

> The children had to choose their own groups. They got into rugby style group holds of their own accord, which was a very bonding and tactile gesture, as sometimes they won't even hold hands. (Teacher Year3)

The children contributed similar insights. They articulated some of their increasing confidence and abilities at being in a public space.

> It was good to work in a group. We can listen to each others' ideas. (Year 3 child)

> I liked it when my stage design was used for the puppet show. (Year 5 child)

> I liked learning how to speak out. (Year 5 Child)

The sessions with the artists may have fostered their confidence when in a public space, able to contribute or not, as they chose. And this confidence appeared to spill over into other public spaces in the school, such as classrooms and playground.

The action research (3) Children's Voices and Choices

Rufford is a nursery and infant school for children aged 3 to 7. Judy Berry is the headteacher and Anne Holt the Creative Partnerships coordinator for the school. Their theme was: 'Children's Voices and Choices: How even very young children can learn to express their wishes, and then have them realised through arts projects'. The research was an action inquiry consisting of a series of long taped conversations between Judy, Anne, various other teachers and Morwenna. The first of these had been intended as just a preliminary interview in which the directions of the action inquiry were collaboratively established. In the event, the conversation was so interesting that it set the pattern for the inquiry. Conversations were held each half term, and lasted for over an hour. Each one was taped and transcribed.

We began by focusing generally on questions about learning in the arts in the Creative Partnerships scheme. These questions were progressively refined, as we worked discursively and reflectively to identify incidents which had been critical when reflecting about children's work with sculptors and dancers — and then to make explicit why these incidents had seemed to be critical. The theme of voices and choices emerged. After this more conversations were held. Further evidence was provided by photographs taken by the children and by documentation ranging from a poem by a school cook, to formal evaluations by outsiders. By Easter, it became clear how the little stories and reflections were able to encapsulate the school's pedagogical principles – and how those principles had clarified through the process of the inquiry.

The inquiry underlined the centrality of Voices and Choices in how the school works. The evidence shows how even very young children, even when they have special needs, can learn to express their collective wishes and then have them realised through planning and executing arts projects. For instance, in one conversation it was decided to include the teacher who had most recently arrived at the school, five years previously, to see if we could identify how staff learned this way of working. She said:

> When Jude first told me what this was about, I said, 'That's going to be quite difficult, because that's just how we are, and it's hard to think back.'

It was this teacher, Helen, who was the subject of one of the little stories told by Judy and Anne, encapsulating the meaning of Voices and Choices for this school:

> Helen is one of the teachers in Class 3. She had got it into her head that because next term we are doing structures anyway – this is part of the half term plan. So she was thinking bridges or arches, I think. She wanted to do something similar to that and then the children cut across it and said they didn't want an arch, they wanted a definite bridge and they knew where they wanted it. So that is what is going to happen and it is going to have lights! Because they feel that they have missed out on lights at the moment because there are two classrooms at the moment with wonderful sculptures both of which are *lit*! (laughs). So this half term we are doing light and next half term we are doing structures, but the children will not forget, you see, that they haven't had the light bit and that's what they are doing this week, aren't they? So it won't be in the hall. It will be in their own classroom and *it will be lit*!

As a result of carrying out the inquiry, the school as a whole gained a better understanding of the pedagogical principles and practices it operates, and which are key in developing Voices and Choices throughout the school. The understanding of how the arts-based work contributed became clearer and stronger. It was obvious that it engaged the children's imaginations and emotions, thus making the exercise of voice and choice more meaningful for them. One outcome of the action inquiry was a leaflet which succinctly explained the rationale behind the arts-based learning for the benefit of anyone coming into the school, be they parents or inspectors.

Each theme in its different way demonstrates how children and young people are helped to learn to participate in public spaces. The themes are described discretely, because that is how the research was structured, although separating them out like this might make them appear more different than they are. But all three schools have all three themes. Indeed it seems that this is no accident. Each theme reinforces the others. Fertile Ground does not apply just in Shepherd. A focus on Children on the Edge does not appear just in Seagrave. Voices and Choices are significant beyond Rufford.

Entering Public Spaces: implications for social justice in schools

The action research projects helped to formulate a question about how pupils learn to be in public spaces instead of staying on the margins. Philosophers have largely ignored such questions. Mainstream political philosophy tends to assume that rational discussion occurs in the civic space which is open to all, and that this is the place where deliberative democracy occurs. Further, it tends to assume that if there is a public space, all citizens are equally able to use it. Finally, it tends to assume that creating public spaces is not something citizens need to learn to do. Educational theorists, too, have largely ignored these questions. The assumption is generally that if a public space is such that pupils' comments are legitimated, they will feel able to participate. This chapter argues that this assumption should be questioned. Some pupils need to learn how to be present in a public space, before they can make decisions about whether or not to join in.

There are implications for schools and for their part in education for social justice. The issue explored in this chapter is not a general one about social justice in and for education. It is not even about voice and how pupils might contribute to the curriculum or management of their schools. Rather, it is about the very possibility of exercising voice – or choosing not to exercise it. It is now possible to see that it is not enough to create spaces where children can express themselves. The research suggests that it is helpful for pupils to be in an environment of mutual respect and mutual learning. It appears that some pupils need to learn how to be fully present in particular public spaces before they can learn that their active presence might enable them to influence what happens. It seems that some pupils need to learn how to exercise voice and choice in one space, before they can exercise them in other spaces. Further, it may be that without the experience of exercising voice and agency, a child – or an adult – can have difficulty believing they have the capacity to do it at all.

These are fundamental issues for education for social justice. Arts-based projects in schools are one way of creating spaces where children learn to be and to express themselves, and can then extend that experience into other public spaces in the school.

The research indicates how education for social justice – for democracy – can reach *all* the children, not just the confident and articulate ones. Schools councils, and various modes of citizenship education, important as they might be, are not enough. Indeed, if only some children are able to join in such structures, they can contribute to the social exclusion of the less confident and articulate children. Such structures certainly remain useful, but they need to be underpinned by strategies to include all children, and the experience of having voice and agency, which can then be exercised.

All this is unlikely to occur in a narrow curriculum, taught narrowly, however good the school's attainment in standardised tests might be. Young people need an education that enables them to learn social justice by doing it. So public spaces have to be created which will give them the experience of exercising voice and choice. The wider hope is that having learned by doing, these young people can use their learning to widen social justice beyond the school into the other institutions of society, in which they find themselves, and in so doing, further social justice in their communities.

Note
Our thanks to *The British Journal of Educational Studies* for permission to publish this shortened version of an article published in the *Journal*, Volume 54 (3) 2006: *Special Issue on Social Justice*.

5
Writing and reading in a multicultural classroom

Gitte Holten Ingerslev
Associate Professor at the Department of Curriculum
Research, Danish University of Education

This study investigates how interpretive reading skills and literary understanding can be enhanced by giving children narrative writing tasks before moving on to a literary text. The class in question in Denmark has many children of migrant workers. They belong to the group of so-called 'hyphenated Danes', they are Danish-Pakistani, Danish-Turkish etc. They belong to what is called an ethnic linguistic minority. The few students of indigenous Danish origin all come from backgrounds with scant tradition for reading fiction. The study also aimed to investigate a possible relation between the students' conception of learning and of reading and interpreting literary texts on the subject of Danish literature, in order to give teachers broader insight into the underlying factors in writing and reading on the one hand and conceptions of learning in a multicultural classroom on the other (Boulton-Lewis *et al*, 2001; Marton, Dall'Alba and Beaty 1993).

The background: The percentage of young people opting for Danish upper secondary school has tripled over the last 20 years, resulting in a much wider range of student backgrounds. In addition, a growing percentage of the young students come from a non-Danish background, yet teaching has not changed radically. The teaching of language and literature in Danish upper secondary schools is still directed towards a small percentage in every class: the students who are already sophisticated language users and experienced readers. The possible consequence is that the inexperienced readers feel defeated and lose interest in language and literature and consequently tend not to establish personal reading strategies.

The research described is based on classroom observations, open interviews with teachers and students, and questionnaires with open-ended questions on learning and reading. The research method is a phenomenographic analysis of students' and teachers' conceptions of learning and the conflicting aims in reading and teaching literature that result from different conceptions of learning.

The study

The study aimed to investigate how reading skills in a multicultural classroom can be enhanced through narrative writing tasks designed especially for students with a simple learning conception.

The study design consisted of:

- classroom observations over three weeks
- teacher interview
- student questionnaire with open questions on learning and reading
- students completing narrative writing tasks before reading literature.

The study produced unexpected results and provided thought-provoking insight into the stressful and burdened life of young immigrants in Danish upper secondary schools. This unpredicted finding added an important aspect to the study.

Different aspects of the class in question

The school where this study took place is situated in the suburbs of a big city. Over the years its student intake has changed, and for various reasons most are now young people from immigrant families.

The students in the class studied provided quite a few challenges for their teachers. There were internal conflicts, students were being bullied, and a good many troublemakers seemed to be concentrated in this particular class. Its students had for example put detergent in the school aquarium, and the fish had died. Some students disliked the biology teacher and decided to smear soap on the floor outside the biology class to make her slip and fall. There were several incidents of fighting among the boys in the class. A group of students, both boys and girls, were silent and kept to themselves, whereas others were boisterous and challenging. There were a great many tensions in the class.

The headteacher had had talks with certain students and their parents on various occasions. In several cases these talks had serious consequences for the student, because their parents punished them for behaving badly at school. The parents had ambitions for their children to have a good education and do well in Danish society. These ambitions seemed to impose a heavy load on many students, and fear of parental reproach and punishment were often part of the students' daily school life. All in all, the students were troubled by many conflicting demands, and their reactions troubled the teachers and the school.

Different approaches to learning
One of the areas that created difficulties for these students was that their conceptions of learning did not correlate with the demands of upper secondary school. This situation was not acknowledged nor explicitly mentioned by either the teachers or the students. This is not surprising as this aspect of teaching and learning is seldom investigated. Research in this area has mainly been carried out within phenomenographic research. It was started in the late seventies by Ference Marton and Roger Säljö at Gothenburg University (Marton, 1979; Säljö, 1979 a, 1979 b, 1979 c). Most of the students in this study demonstrated an unsophisticated learning conception. The categories of learning conceptions are developed in phenomenographic research, which investigates the variation of conceptions within particular areas. Further details are available on page http://www.ped.gu.se/biorn/phgraph/welcome.html (Marton,

Dall'Alba and Beaty, 1993; Biggs, 1987; Marton and Booth, 1997). This research deals with six categories of learning conceptions. The first three are:

To learn is

- ■ to get more knowledge
- ■ to remember
- ■ to be able to use.

Students who hold any of these conceptions of learning are more likely to come from non-reading backgrounds and to feel insecure and ill at ease when starting in upper secondary school, especially with the humanistic, interpretive subjects. They will often say 'Just write on the blackboard what I'm supposed to say at my exam'. Thus they are 'Certainty Orientated' as opposed to 'Uncertainty Orientated' in their study approach (Huber *et al*, 1992).

The remaining three conceptions are categorised like this:

To learn is

- ■ to understand
- ■ to change one's knowledge
- ■ to change as a person.

Students who hold any of these latter conceptions of learning would typically be probing, investigative, uncertainty orientated students who want to understand the content of the subject. They would typically want to do project based, decentralised work which would challenge their habitual thinking and enhance their development.

The distribution of learning conceptions in the class under study is depicted in figure 1 opposite.

Ten students demonstrate an unsophisticated learning conception, defining learning as an accumulation of facts put into their heads by a teacher or a book. They typically read things again and again until they knew them by heart. This learning conception makes great demands of the teachers, as they are then burdened with the responsibility for the learning that takes place in class. If students learn nothing, it means they have a bad teacher.

Figure 1. Learning Conceptions

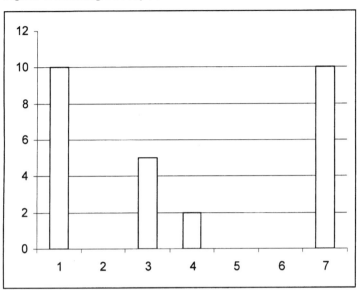

1. Learning Conception 1: *to get more knowledge*
2. Learning Conception 2: *to remember*
3. Learning Conception 3: *to be able to use*
4. Learning Conception 4: *to understand*
5. Learning Conception 5: *to change one's knowledge*
6. Learning Conception 6: *to change as a person*
7.To get a good future – *to be a success*

Five of the students declared that if one can use knowledge for school purposes, one has learned the material, while two wrote that they have learned the material if they can *understand* it. The idea that one has learned something when one is able to understand shows that the students' focus has shifted. Learning is no longer about a teacher being able to put knowledge into the heads of the students – it is about the students being able to combine the new knowledge with what they already know in order to build new understanding.

Interestingly, no less than ten students answered the question: *What does it mean to learn something?* by writing things like: to get a good future, to build a good future, to become a success, to get a job. I have done such small scale research in many Danish classrooms but

Figure 2. An average class

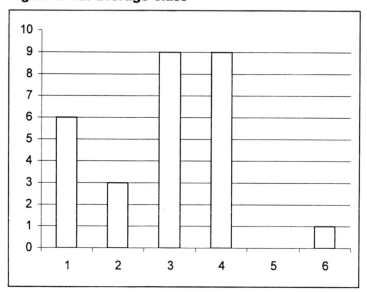

1. Learning Conception 1: *to get more knowledge*
2. Learning Conception 2: *to remember*
3. Learning Conception 3: *to be able to use*
4. Learning Conception 4: *to understand*
5. Learning Conception 5: *to change one's knowledge*
6. Learning Conception 6: *to change as a person*

I have never received that answer before. The answers may be due to a linguistic problem but they might also reveal the fact that it is stressful to be a young immigrant in a country that has not yet fully accepted you, but is waiting to see if you will manage, just as your expectant parents are waiting.

If you asked the same question in an average class, you would get answers like those shown above in Figure 2.

The distribution of answers in this class is more even, and it is likely that the students will challenge each other, as approximately one third want to *understand* the material. Furthermore, the students with learning conceptions 1-3 are likely to change gradually through exchanges with and challenges from their teachers and fellow students in a dialogic classroom.

The distribution of learning conceptions among the research group showed that the class was far more homogenous than expected, both in their learning conceptions and their reading experience. Thus there were no distinctive differences between the students and it was not possible to demonstrate a clear relation between their conception of learning and their reading and interpreting of literary texts. Consequently it is more useful to highlight the unexpected insight the study gave into how inexperienced readers with unsophisticated learning conceptions can benefit from narrative writing tasks.

Writing tasks and interpretation skills

The students who took part in this study were going to read a novel by a young Danish author, and by way of introduction were given the following writing tasks to complete over 90 minutes:

- *Where does your story take place?* Use your senses, think of a location outside or inside. What does it look like? Smell, view, sounds etc.
- *When?* What time of the day, and of the year? Light, darkness, weather?
- *Who?* Three people are present: who are they? Age, looks, characteristics?
- *What?* Choose a theme, e.g. love, revenge, money and design a conflict
- *The culmination.* Write the main scene in your story.

The idea was that the students should contemplate how to write a precise description of a place, of an atmosphere, of a person, of a conflict and that they should consider what made a piece of text work by doing it themselves. Knowing this should make them better readers when they tackled the novel. They were asked to write according to the principle *show it; don't tell it* – and were given some short examples and exercises before they started on the task.

All the students seemed to like the task, and after a few minutes of talk and questions everybody wrote enthusiastically. To my surprise most of the stories the students wrote were filled with anxiety and dread. Two boys and two girls wrote stories that resembled **night-**

mares. In one, two brothers are on their way to the hospital where their sister is giving birth. Their car breaks down, the bus is delayed, there is no bike in sight. When they finally manage to get there they are told that the baby had survived but that their sister died. The narrator faints. The two brothers in the story are unable to act. No matter what they do, they are blocked in their efforts.

In another story, two girls who are friends are spending a cosy evening together. They are happily setting out sweets and deciding what film to watch. One girl leaves the room to fetch something, and suddenly the other girl hears a strange sound and realises that her friend's mother, who has been missing for months, is lying in the next room beaten almost to death. The horror and dread are intense and the story ends unresolved. Thus an apparently uncomplicated and pleasant situation turns out to be filled with dread just beneath the surface.

The theme of **identity crisis** characterised the stories of four of the girls. They wrote about feeling like a Dane but not looking like one and not being treated like one in Danish society, or about looking like a Pakistani girl, being treated like one but not feeling like one while visiting their families in Pakistan.

In three girls' stories the narrators are **criminals** who committed a crime, were discovered and are now in danger.

Two boys and one girl took the theme of **amnesia**. The narrators are caught in terrible dark places. They do not know how they got there. There is a strange smell. There is something sticky, thick on the floor – is it blood? There is an unintelligible, incomprehensible sound nearby etc. etc. The descriptions are filled with dread and disorientation.

Illness features in the stories by three of the girls. The narrators have just been told that they are mortally ill and will soon die. They are sorrowful and afraid to tell their parents, who will be very distressed. They have to carry their burden alone.

To sum up, the stories typically had protagonists who felt unable to act. Beneath every situation, however pleasant it appeared to be, a danger might be hidden. Nothing is what it seems to be. The protagonists are disorientated and carry terrible secrets.

Some of the stories were read aloud in class to demonstrate their good stylistic and linguistic qualities, and one student pointed out that all the stories seemed to be about with fear. Another student answered: '*No wonder, most people are afraid most of the time, aren't they?*' Nobody contradicted him. The consensus was that he was right. The fearful themes of the stories may well be an indication of how these young immigrants feel about their situation in Denmark and the school system, and especially about the subject of Danish literature. All the national literature refers to cultural and historically based conventions, so this area is difficult to navigate if you belong to a different cultural background. It was interesting that all the students were good writers – their texts were skilfully written and made fascinating reading.

After this writing session, the class read and interpreted the Danish novel. They returned to their writing experience while interpreting the text: *This person does not come alive, there are many details missing or this place does not seem real – why are we not told about...?*

The students had undoubtedly become more alert readers because of the writing sessions. Furthermore, their appetite for reading and understanding a text was enhanced by their having been allowed to write about their own anxiety. There was much interest in this short but promising project exploring learning conceptions and reading backgrounds in the class. It revealed that writing tasks functioned as a motivational factor and revealed potential in a class which in many ways was malfunctioning and predominantly ill at ease about reading Danish literature.

Two factors seem to have played an important role in the students' changed motivation: firstly their feeling of ownership – they owned their stories, which were private and important to them – and secondly, their success as writers. It was obvious that these short texts were poignant and well written, and this gave the students the feeling that for once they understood a little of what this difficult subject was all about.

The teachers of classes made up of students such as those in the study face a difficult task, as they have to get to know the circumstances and views of each student before they can establish fruitful collaboration.

Perspectives

In Danish upper secondary education the ideal is to be able to educate young readers to enjoy reading literature and develop a critical sense of what they read. The requirements echo the Danish way of thinking about education and cultural ideals. The underlying demands create a feeling of exhaustion and lack of energy in many young inexperienced readers, among them many of the young immigrants, because they cannot understand the precise requirements of the subject.

On the other hand, the students with foreign backgrounds know that education is the only access to success and stability in the country in which they have settled so they work as hard as possible to fulfil the demands. It is their only way to avoid marginalisation. It is hard for them to obtain an education, and Danish literature is the most difficult subject of all.

Despite the change in student uptake in upper secondary education in Denmark, the number of students from families with little formal education who obtain a university degree has scarcely changed (Hansen, 1995). The reasons for this are multiple. For a start, these young people are not given access to the requisite cultural codes (Bruner, 1998).

The subject of Danish Language and Literature has significant potential for building access to cultural tools so that students can take a wider and more reflective perspective on their lives and their own role in determining them.

For this reason it is of utmost importance that the central issues of language and literature form a never-ending dialogue in students' consciousness. The starting point is the recognition by teachers of all students' potential. Students must be supported in working at their own pace and helped gradually to change and develop their learning conceptions, learning strategies and personal insight. Sadly, this is not always the case. But this approach is important for political, sociological and humanistic reasons, and this chapter will, we hope, generate discussion.

6

Teaching teachers cooperative learning: an intercultural challenge

Francesca Gobbo

Professor of Intercultural Education and Anthropology
of Education, University of Turin, Italy

Introduction

Contemporary societies, and their inhabitants' identities, are like an ever moving flux, so that people can no longer make sense of and act in their everyday life according to the widely shared cultural and social criteria learned through the enculturation process and stable relationships (Bauman, 2003). Because of accelerated historical discontinuity, cosmopolitanism is today being interpreted as: 'both the presupposition and the result of a conceptual reconfiguration of our modes of perception' (Beck, 2006:2). Societies have become aware of the historical changes that result from the dislocation and relocation of individuals and families because of the worldwide disparities in the quality of life, work opportunities and possibility of survival, and also the urgent need to answer the new conditions effectively and creatively.

Italy is no exception. Mobility and change have affected its demography and work sectors, and induced a new sense of social responsibility among a sizable part of its population. Legal immigrants now account for 4.5 per cent of the total population, which indicates a significant turn in the overall social composition and identity of the country. The unforeseen passage from a country of emigration to one of immigration has become a reality.

This does not mean that the transition has been smooth, as the news too often reminds us. However, the discourse of intercultural education has played an important role in pointing out, reducing and preventing prejudicial attitudes towards newly arrived pupils, and in assigning a publicly positive meaning to diversity. Diversity has always been a component of Italian society in terms of linguistic, religious, ethnic and class differences, but until recently mostly in the private realm and usually ignored or discounted in the public one such as the education system (Gobbo, 2003, 2004, 2066, 2007). Italian schools and teachers have sought and promoted educational approaches capable of responding to increasingly heterogeneous classrooms through the recognition and valorisation of differences.

Intercultural education and cooperative learning: the background

Because such approaches require *ad hoc* in-service training programmes, many local administrations have founded and supported Intercultural Centres in the last twenty years. These aim to provide teachers with much needed intercultural knowledge and skills through courses on the immigrants' cultures and religions and an array of didactic projects as well as festive encounters between immigrant families and schools or the local population.

Two years ago the Bologna Intercultural Centre invited me to give a course on Elizabeth Cohen's version of cooperative learning, known as Complex Instruction (Cohen, 1994; Cohen and Lotan, 1997) and I eagerly accepted. I hoped to help the teachers recognise that when it is connected with low social status, diversity will be negatively perceived. And this produces low expectations towards the school achievement of such children and significantly inhibits their peers' interactions with them even in group work.

Complex Instruction explicitly aims to answer the needs, wishes and hopes of the heterogeneous classrooms of today and to attain equity in education by changing teachers' and peers' expectations towards pupils of low status. In the words of Elizabeth Cohen:

> the purpose of the program is the creation of equitable classrooms. These are classrooms where all students have access to challenging curricula, where students all participate equally in cooperative learning, helping each other to grasp difficult concepts and to solve problems, and where almost all of the students are successful in academic performance. (2003:153)

This educational strategy originated at Stanford University, the result of over twenty years of research and development by a group of educational, sociological and psychological researchers:

> the model has its theoretical roots in sociological analysis of the social system of the classroom. Key features of this social system are the nature of the classroom tasks, the roles of the students and teachers, and the patterns of interaction among students and between students and teachers. These are the features that are often responsible for failure of students in traditional classrooms. Alternatively, changing these features can change the situation so that many more students can be successful. (*ibid*)

To enable 'all children to learn', by seeing 'all children as smart', requires an understanding of 'the forces outside and inside the classroom that create inequity among students'- the traditional domain of sociologists of education. In Complex Instruction, sociological theory and research were eventually used 'to design and evaluate interventions to promote equitable classrooms' (*ibid*). The strategy structures group work around didactic units centred on multiple abilities, and requires teachers to delegate authority to pupils and give them detailed feedback on group work dynamics. Diversity in the classroom has to be seen and treated in terms of inequality. Recognising that students of low status can bring their own intellectual abilities and skills to the learning process is an act of social justice, and it gives these students the opportunity to contribute to the task set for the group (Cohen, 2003; Lotan, 2003, 2006a, 2006b).

Though Complex Instruction predates intercultural education, it has a powerful intercultural dimension. It works with students' different cultural, linguistic and cognitive abilities as resources for the learning achieved when every student participates equally in group work. And they can contribute in their particular way to understanding difficult concepts and solving open ended problems (Batelaan and Van Hoof, 1996; Batelaan ed., 1998; Gobbo, 2000). Precisely for these reasons, Complex Instruction was chosen for a European Commission's Socrates Programme aimed at developing 'equitable, cooperative classrooms' and 'intercultural learning processes, thereby providing equity for all students, regardless of their cultural and social background' (Batelaan, 1998:5).

Teaching teachers Cooperative Learning: some initial issues and questions

The Bologna teachers on the course were eager to widen their already considerable educational knowledge and skills, and to learn a new way of doing group work (Gobbo *et al*, 2005). The course was certainly successful in terms of attendance, participation and discussion[1]. The teachers acknowledged the social and relational disparities in their classrooms, and highlighted the difficulty in coping in ways that enabled every pupil to learn. They had practised a loose form of group work in their classrooms from time to time but had noticed how the children had perceived it almost as a break from the predominant teaching style, in which the teacher dispenses instructions and guides pupils through tasks.

The teachers recognised that group work had usually been very informal, leading to noise and confusion in the classroom. They were aware that only some students busied themselves with the task while the rest of the group looked on. But when every student wanted to contribute to the task, conflicts and tensions almost always arose, so that most children disliked working together and strongly preferred working under the teacher's reassuring maternal direction and supervision.

At the end of the course, some of the teachers expressed interest in learning more about Complex Instruction so they could construct two original didactic units of their own to test later in their diverse classrooms. One teacher aimed to go from abstract understanding and appreciation of Cohen's strategy to actually implementing it. The teachers felt challenged by the task of combining the multiple abilities criterion with their own educational objectives that took into account the pupils' characteristics.

After lengthy discussions, the teachers who stuck to their initial plan decided to develop the first unit around the idea of point of view, for the younger children, and the second, for the older pupils, around the idea of communication and misunderstanding. I arranged to meet with them once a month until late Spring 2005, when the two units were tested twice in five classrooms – one first grade, two second grade, one third grade and one fifth grade. Isabella Pescarmona, a former student of mine, and I observed how these teachers had explained and organised the group work and how the pupils went about working cooperatively.

Complex Instruction in Bologna classrooms: the teachers' reflective views

After testing the two units of Complex Instruction, additional meetings were held to discuss the experience and what we had learned from it. Some groups had completed the task successfully, thanks to their capacity to make the most of every pupil's arguments and suggestions and to propose creative solutions that surprised and even moved the adult observers, such as a poignant response to the tsunami tragedy. Or the withdrawn and usually silent 7 year old Albanian child, who showed unexpected creative and reflective abilities that enabled the tasks to be completed – which propelled him into the role of inspiring, resourceful and dynamic referent for the rest of the group.

Other groups had been unable to complete the tasks, mostly because of conflicts, pupils refusing to participate in group work, and prejudicial attitudes towards contributions by low status pupils. In one significant case, a child certified as a slow learner had been the only one to understand what the group had been asked to do, but his low social and academic status prevented him from receiving attention from the others in the group. Cohen (1994, 2003) observed that this is not uncommon in heterogeneous classrooms: they can indeed isolate pupils of low status from their classmates. So this has to be counteracted by the teachers in their detailed and specific feedback on group work.

Perhaps not unexpectedly, the Bologna teachers appreciated the strong connection made in Complex Instruction between the didactic units' activities and the curriculum. But they pointed to the different kinds of problems encountered in their classrooms, and the additional educational goals they therefore had to set. Their articulate reflections on the teacher's educational role in relation to the rapidly changing classroom and society suggested that the pursuit of equity should also take account of this existential dimension.

As the analysis went on, it revealed that testing their units had been a litmus test: the teachers were surprised at how they had taken the culture of their school for granted (Florio-Ruane, 1996; Gobbo, 2000). It is this culture that shapes their customary way of teaching and organising learning activities, and also their interaction with the pupils and their expectations. For instance, they acknowledged how difficult it had been for them to delegate authority to the groups and refrain from rushing to their aid whenever a doubtful or frustrated pupil summoned them.

Earlier in the course I had discussed the reasons for classroom co-operation. I reminded the teachers that Italian educational thought and practice has a respectable tradition of group work that has always envisaged learning in groups as a way to learn, and valued democratic participation in decision making processes and solidarity. By the end of the course it was clear that it had inaugurated a long and exciting season of educational debates and didactic innovation among Italian teachers whose main goal had been equality of education.

The comparative perspective I briefly cast on Complex Instruction was meant to problematise Cohen's educational innovation so it would not become an instructional package or recipe to be delivered 'in the nick of time'. It was meant to query the transferability of educational ideas and strategies from one social, cultural and political context (the USA) to another one (in this case Italy), and recognise how much creative interpretation was needed. In times of globalisation, there are many similarities between different social and educational contexts and this will foster borrowing and disseminating new concepts, approaches and goals in the belief that because there are common problems, there can be common solutions. I would argue that this modernist belief ignores the need for imported ideas and programmes to encounter and interact with the social, historical and intellectual fabrics they are supposed to innovate.

I like to think that the respect for diversity that intercultural education promotes is made more meaningful because the disseminators of this educational innovation relate not only to institutional contexts and teaching traditions but above all to the people whose complex professional identity makes them vital as partners in an intercultural dialogue.

Exploring the research question through reflective conversations

Learning about and experimenting with Complex Instruction brought a fresh professional awareness to the Bologna teachers that generated not only new educational knowledge and skills but, more importantly, the realisation that this knowledge had been sown in cultivated ground. Their surprise and awareness, which was greater than I had anticipated, suggested that the course and the classroom testing was a special intercultural encounter that merited exploration through reflective conversations.

The conversations took place immediately after the classroom testing[2]. I sought to learn from these teachers how what they had just accomplished related to their learning and professional experience and to their personal choices and educational goals. My initial goal was to determine how much the migration of educational ideas and strategies from one social, cultural and political context to another is understood and creatively interpreted in the new environment through professional and cultural perspectives that stem from, and respond to, internal concerns. The teachers' stories about their personal and professional choices and investments, including their stories of why they attended this course, show that they see themselves as agents, not mere consumers, of educational innovations, and as active, thoughtful mediators between their own historically contextualised cultural, educational and political ideas, and changing public and private realities.

Silvia, the 5th grade teacher, spoke of her five years with the same class – which tested the unit on communication – as an educational journey during which she had sought to promote the children's capability to make decisions and choices of their own, and their willingness to cooperate with each other. One of her major educational goals – to make children independent learners and reflective moral beings – had seemed well supported, even enhanced, by the Complex Instruction approach to group work. Silvia emphasised repeatedly how she had paid special attention to the classroom's interaction dynamics and tried to understand them against the background of social, cultural and demographic changes. Many of her pupils are their family's only child, so they grow up more comfortable with adults than with other children. Being in the company of their peers can provoke deep frustration or feelings of vulnerability, inadequacy and unhappiness that undermine their ability to learn. A teacher cannot ignore such feelings lest she lose those pupils, and she will increasingly have to act as facilitator or conflict mediator to favour learning.

Not only is the Italian family changing but so is the school itself: activities and projects that were educationally effective ten or fifteen years ago no longer seem to be so, and new ideas and tools must be devised to meet the challenge of the 'current revolution'. Silvia finds Complex Instruction especially relevant: it prompts teachers to reflect, be organised and learn to withstand time and curriculum metaphorical pressures. Its educational goals are open to discussion and related to a way of organising group work based on scientific theory and research which provides procedural indications, rather than on ideology.

Silvia's believes that Complex Instruction might be 'a healthy shock' for colleagues captivated by instructional routines, whose educational creativity has declined due to the belief that continuity in teaching habits and activities saves a precious and scarce resource such as time, whereas most educational innovations require more time. But because Cohen's strategy opens and problematises 'teachers' educational horizons', it raises issues such as the relation between children's social status and learning, or the question of teachers' authority, and goals such as equity.

Silvia recalled the 'heroic times when her teaching career had started: the 'battle for *tempo pieno*' (full time school) was the emblem of educational progressivism and the worst confrontations between conservative and progressive families and teachers were over, but the memory of them, and of the 'open classrooms' continued to stir parents and beginning teachers. Silvia sees striking similarities between the 1970s and today: things are changing just as quickly as thirty years ago when progressive educational innovations were seen as the way to ensure equality of education. So, after wondering why she had devoted so much of her free time to constructing the didactic unit with the other teachers, she decided that it allowed her the opportunity to reaffirm both the educational hopes and goals of a new social order, and the crucial relevance of values such as social solidarity.

Silvia did not think that Complex Instruction was 'culturally situated', but observed that the teachers' concern for children's existential dimension is not considered in Cohen's educational strategy, perhaps because of the differences between school and family contexts in the United States and Italy. Such strategy thus needs be complemented by further reflections and research on children's relational difficulties and peers' conflicts and tensions.

In 2004, Valeria was a 2nd grade teacher in a school at the foot of the Appennines, almost an hour from Bologna. Like Silvia, she had welcomed Complex Instruction for its relevance to changing times, its focus on equity, the neatly designed structure of group work and the strong connection to the curriculum, its scientific basis. She praised it, contrasting it with earlier European approaches to cooperative work and learning, and recollecting the Italian historical context of the 1970s. Though just a child, she remembers the 'years of a great educational revolution' whose aims were to establish *tempo pieno* and promote parents' participation in school life. *Tempo pieno* answered a social demand but had soon to reinvent itself in educational terms: thus teachers fostered group work as well as pedagogical activism and questioned the authority of textbooks by having pupils make their own.

Valeria started to teach in the mid-1980s, when the law that re-organised school's classroom teaching and curricula had been voted in Parliament after intense debates among teachers. Their voice had been listened to and valued by the Ministry of Education, unlike in the case of the 2004 school reform, that 'arrived already neatly packaged, a matter of 'take it or leave it'. She is active in intercultural education projects planned and supported by the Bologna Inter-cultural Centre and she picked up the underlying intercultural dimension of Complex Instruction: it gives equal dignity and respect to different ways of learning and communicating as well as attribut-ing a specific role to each group member to facilitate their visibility and cooperation in solving the task and being firmly rooted in the curriculum. She shared Silvia's concerns for classroom interaction difficulties: some children don't want to play with certain class-mates, don't want to stand beside them in line, walk with them. The excluded ones

> suffer tremendously, they are frustrated and ask adults for help, [since] they do not know how to cope with frustration or overcome it. And they are also frustrated when their school performance does not meet their expectations or their parents', who find it difficult to accept their children's difficulties and uneasiness.

About the conflicts and tensions arising during group work, Valeria sounded more optimistic than Silvia. She observed that:

> group work takes place in a protected environment, there are all the conditions for the conflict to become 'thought provoking' and [per-haps] give way to better task results. Even when this doesn't happen, group work functions as a litmus test: it brings out the hidden ten-sions, but in a positive way since it gives [both the children and the teacher] the opportunity to discuss [the feelings against coopera-tion]. And this can happen with the help of the teacher.

Valeria had learned a lot about herself while testing the didactic unit: in particular she realised how hard it was to let pupils work or fail by themselves. She interpreted her anxious attitude in terms of the school culture: as a teacher, she tends to mediate a lot, providing her pupils 'with a sort of predigested fare'. That they were 7 years old at the time might explain her behaviour; yet from her further reflec-tions it can be gathered that it is not just a matter of age:

I tend to answer their queries. It saves time as well, if you only have an hour [for a certain educational activity], you speed up things by making the exercise simpler. They do it more quickly. [All that's needed is that] you skip some steps ... Let's face it: what hurts in Complex Instruction is delegation of authority; there is a real suffering on the part of the teacher.

She found what Complex Instruction expected her to do as a teacher both a trial and an experiment. But she could think of a reason for her feelings:

I believe in the [importance of the] emotional aspect of the teaching relationship, because of the age of children. And if there were an outside expert, I would want to show that the children can do well. Maybe it is related to a certain notion of professional competence: in the sense that I must not fail to provide children an with answer ... they can trust me.

In 2004 Elena taught science and mathematics to 3rd graders. The school is in a small town in the middle of the flat farming country between Bologna and Ferrara. Complex Instruction had reassured her that students could work in group and complete learning tasks without raising too many problems of interaction dynamics. Both times that she tested the didactic unit she had collaborated to create, she sounded fairly satisfied with the relational results – although observers would describe the classroom as far from quiet. Like her colleagues, Elena appreciated the connection between the group tasks and the curriculum because her goal is 'to try and explain curricular topics through group work'. Discipline problems seemed to grow worse when she adopted a didactic teaching style, so she hoped that cooperative learning would be more successful[3], especially as she believed that 'children should learn to compare their different views among themselves, and then reach their own conclusions or solutions'. She was also aware that inequality based on social and cultural differences still prevails in classrooms and is surprised that the goal of equitable classrooms seems no longer to be of concern.

Elena also appreciated the way Complex Instruction need not be employed continuously. This enables teachers to practise it without feeling they are sacrificing precious hours of the annual curriculum plan, about which they 'have become so obsessed'. Knowing that

time for innovative educational activities can be successfully negotiated enhanced these teachers' professional identity. Elena pointed
out how they had been able to reflect critically on their work, goals
and priorities while creating the unit precisely because of the open-
endedness of this cooperative learning strategy. Elena had participated in group work in high school in 1968, a time of student unrest and the root of many cultural and educational changes in
Europe. Group work had been totally new to her and her classmates
but they liked it so much that they would even return to school in the
afternoon to prepare their own science textbook! The group climate
of the time was another crucial feature for her, as she had been
helped by her group to overcome her difficulties.

Marta taught 2nd graders in another school located in the country-
side near Bologna. She too had seen how Complex Instruction's
focus on social justice and equality of education resonated with the
students' and country's unrest in 1968, when she was still in high
school and interested in what was happening around her. But her
main reason for attending the course and collaborating on the construction and testing of the didactic unit was her concern over her
conflict ridden classroom. She had been eager to understand if this
kind of cooperative learning could provide 'principles and tools to
create a friendlier and more tolerant climate among pupils'. She believed that the idea of assigning specific roles and group tasks,
besides the learning task, to each pupil could improve the classroom
climate. Accordingly, she had distributed Complex Instruction's
roles with great care, trying to match them with or challenge
through them the capabilities and status position of every child. Although the learning tasks had eventually been completed with some
success, testing the unit had raised questions: why had there been
such a level of disagreement and quarrelling during group work?
Why had pupils been unable to do in group work what they did in
regular classroom activity, such as playing a skit? Why was it that
pupils used to taking initiative could not do so, or only with great
difficulty, when involved in group work? Marta was not sure how to
answer these questions but she found that being able to discuss her
doubts and uncertainties with outside observers helped her clarify
them to herself.

Conclusions

In this chapter I have tried to weave together the different strands of a complex teaching and learning experience that started as one of many initiatives taken in Italy to promote and support equality of education through intercultural education, and developed into an exploration of teachers' agency and reflective thinking on the process of adopting an innovative educational approach. The belief that educational innovation is especially invented – but also borrowed and disseminated, as in this case – in times of perceived and actual social and cultural change is underlined in the Bologna teachers' narratives and it was certainly their main reason to attend the course during three glorious Spring weekends. But educational innovation is also often developed to reaffirm and realise fundamental human rights such as educational equality, an aim that is clearly at the centre of Elizabeth Cohen's educational strategy and of the teachers' narratives of their personal values and professional concerns.

Their reflections on classroom practice and their caring attention for today children's existential and relational difficulties made these teachers aware that in order to be *educationally* effective, Complex Instruction needs to be theoretically complemented by taking into account peers' problematic interpersonal interactions. These interactions appear to be related not to low social or academic status but rather to the deep structural and relational changes obtaining in the Italian family today. Finally, their thoughtful reflections on earlier times and challenging educational innovations indicate that learning and testing a new and innovative approach never takes place without mobilising a person's own cherished values, together with her professional knowledge, teaching experiences and emotions, and that these act as intercultural mediators as well as creative reinterpreters and reconstructors of what is being learned and practised.

Notes

1 The course was held in a residential structure on the hills outside Bologna, where we met for three weekends in May and June for a total of 36 hours. But conversations about Complex Instruction, pupils and school policies, teachers' educational goals and hopes went on during meals, breaks and free time. More than 30 teachers working in primary and secondary schools enrolled and

though attendance varied depending on school deadlines it never dropped below 30. The course consisted of a presentation of Cohen's educational strategy, followed by group work with Complex Instruction units developed by the Socrates project CLIP (see Batelaan, 1998), simulation of teacher's feedback and discussion of the experience. The final weekend was devoted to the preparation of three Complex Instruction units based on teachers' choice of topic and construction of tasks.

2 Only the narratives of four teachers are presented here. The fifth took place at the end of the school year so there was no time to hold the conversation. The names of the four teachers are fictitious and the texts of the taped, then transcribed, conversations have been edited after being read by the Bologna teachers.

3 After testing their units in 2005, the five teachers planned to construct two new didactic units and resume meetings and discussion on cooperative learning during 2006-2007. Their 2004 experience was presented at the International Conference on Intercultural Education organised in 2005 in Verona by the International Association for Intercultural Education, and the classroom testing was presented at the annual meeting of Intercultural Centres held in Bari in October 2006.

Section III
Constructing identities

7

Crossing boundaries?
Complexities and drawbacks to
gendered success stories

Ann-Sofie Holm
PhD student in Education at University
College of Boras, Sweden
Elisabet Öhrn
Professor of Education at University
College of Boras, Sweden

Conceptual framework

This chapter focuses on two groups of adolescents who seem to do gender in quite successful ways. One group is made up of popular and high-achieving girls, the other of 'immigrant' boys – the word used by the pupils themselves – who emphasise their recent development into pro-school pupil identities. Ways of doing gender within educational settings seem to have become more flexible. Although gender relations may appear stable even seen in the long term view (Delamont, 2001), there are indications of more variation than previously described. This should be seen in relation to changes in the theories and research methods applied (see Öhrn, 2000) so that variation is more emphasised in contemporary gender research. Such variations are further theorised by Connell (1996a) in his analysis of the ways various masculinities and

91

femininities are constructed. Femininities are generally said to be more diverse than masculinities because of differences in the pressure to subordinate to hegemonic forms of gender.

Contemporary empirical research in education also points to the variation of femininities rather than masculinities when discussing presumed changes over time. Proposed 'new' gender patterns emphasise the changing actions of girls – not boys – whether in achievement or behaviour at school. There is no male equivalent to the 'New Girl' proposed by some Nordic educational researchers during the last decade (Öhrn, 2000). The concept of the New Girl was introduced by researchers in the 1990s who found groups of girls acting in more publicly active, extrovert and independent ways in class than usually reported. It has been argued though (Öhrn, 2000) that this is neither a new finding, nor is it typical of contemporary gender research.

As for masculinities in school, markers of status often mentioned by schoolboys are toughness – physical as well as verbal – prowess in sport, competition and (hetero-) sexual interests (see e.g. Connell, 1996b). Often these masculinities are described as antithetical to school achievements. Among girls it seems more expected and acceptable to become a 'swot' (Epstein, 1999) and norms point to being adaptable and attractive (e.g. Frosh et al, 2002). Connell (1996b) points to the particular importance of informal peer cultures for the development of gender relations. The boundaries between the genders are carefully guarded by the group, especially by the boys (Mac an Ghaill, 1994). Violations and 'jokes' are often used to safeguard the norms and unity of the group, but also to demarcate limits for keeping other groups out. Homophobia, sexual harassment and sexist jargon are vehicles for doing this (Osbeck et al, 2003). In order to resist and respond to such actions, social networks and friends are vital (Gordon et al, 2000).

Gender is seen in this chapter as a social construction and humans as doing gender. Both formal schooling and informal groupings are actively involved in the construction of different femininities and masculinities. Gender has different bearings for different social groups, so analysis needs to take account of social class and ethnicity. In Sweden, as elsewhere, pupils themselves consider family background – not least ethnicity – to affect their position and situation in school (Öhrn, 2005). As demonstrated by for instance Mac an Ghaill (1988) in Britain, different groups of 'immigrants' are expected to act and achieve differently in school, and this has a with bearing on the kind of femininities and masculinities likely to develop. Also, gender relations are expected to vary with respect to ethnic groups. Research on ethnicity and racialisation in Sweden has pointed to norms of gender equality as vital for the very construction of Swedishness and hence for understandings of the 'others' (see Öhrn, 2002). Immigrants are stereotyped as largely opposing the norms of gender equality if they are male or, if female, as victims of patriarchal structures in the immigrant culture.

The empirical study

We draw here on an ongoing Swedish project *Young people´s perspectives on their schooling. Emergent femininities and masculinities*, which explores how various groups of pupils experience daily life in school and the ways they do gender. The project includes two schools chosen from contrasting areas; one from a rural area and one from a middle-sized town, with different social structures and social and ethnic relations. The school located in a rural community with barely 20,000 citizens is ethnically homogenous, the other, situated in an ethnically diverse district, has approximately 25 per cent pupils with ethnic origins other than Swedish. From each school, one 9th grade class was selected for the study. In all, 42 pupils (19 girls and 23 boys) aged 15 or16 took part.

Fieldwork in the schools took place in 2003-2004. The data-production included observations during lessons and breaks to observe interactions, peer relations and relations with teachers, with an overall focus on gender processes. Single-sex group interviews were conducted with the pupils, and teachers' views on observations were gathered. One teacher who met the pupils regularly was formally interviewed at the end of the fieldwork.

The pupil interviews focused on specific incidents that had been observed during fieldwork as well as common themes concerning pupils' individual experiences and conceptions of gender in school.

93

To research positions and hierarchies among femininities and masculinities, questions about popularity were thought useful. Methods from international empirical research, in particular Frosh *et al* (2002, see also Phoenix 2004) have provided important points of departure. Phoenix and her colleagues mapped accepted and dominant as well as subordinated positions of masculinity by studying young working class boys' definitions of popularity.

This chapter focuses on two groups of adolescents in the study who seem to do gender in quite successful ways. We especially explore the complexities and implications of the kind of 'success stories' told by the pupils from these groups.

The popular girls

In the rural class (12 girls and 12 boys), most of the pupils live in the same neighbourhood and know each other well. The class seems open and talkative. However, there appears to be a strict hierarchical order among the groups in the class, seemingly related to competitiveness and sportiness. Football appears highly valued both in and outside school. Most of the class engage in various sports, in particular in playing football in the local club.

Positioning in class

One of the groups in the rural school consists of three girls: Susan, Pia (both ethnic Swedes) and Kim Ling (of immigrant background). The group holds a strong position in class and, according to the interviews, is generally seen as the most popular at school. The girls seem socially extrovert, good-looking, competitive, self-confident and successful in sports as well as schoolwork – attributes highly valued by the class. The girls admit to being quite talkative and dominating in lessons. According to the field notes, the top set girls tend to be popular with the adults at school. Teachers show great trust and confidence in them and sometimes consult them about democratic or relational dilemmas in school.

Although a few of their classmates voice some dissatisfaction with the girls and perceive them as snobs, their status is acknowledged by most of the class. Jonna and Yasmine, the least popular girls in the class, express their admiration of the popular girls:

Jonna: They dress in a special way.

Yasmine: They talk to everybody. They are really kind and nice.

Jonna: And they talk in a special way that makes you completely captured by them. Susan certainly has her own way of doing things. I guess that's why all the boys fall in love with her. They [the popular girls] have their own special style, they are very special.

Social relations are important for establishing a strong position in the class and the three girls stress their interpersonal relationships. Their group seems pretty much closed to other girls in class and the popular girls declare that they rather prefer joining in with the group of popular boys. This alliance seems to reinforce and strengthen the prestige and status of both parties. The popular boys and girls hang about together during breaks; they sometimes work together during lessons and have friendly physical contact, like hugging and caressing. This kind of cross-gender 'networking' is described by the girls as a pleasurable way to get closer to others, and that it gives them strength to speak up in class.

Judging from the observations it might be that the popular girls and boys have developed fluent, less fixed forms of masculinity and femininity. The relations and behaviours in the top set tend to be more cross-gendered compared to other groups in the study. At the same time, both groups stress individual 'female' and 'male' features in physical appearance and emphasise their heterosexual interests. The flirting between the girls and boys in the top set might be seen as confirming their success in a heterosexual market, which helps them establish a strong position. It might also be seen as emphasising heteronormativity, which – according to interviews as well as field notes – appeared uncontested in these settings.

Football

Although sporty girls are shown to be viewed in the literature on physical education and gender (Paechter and Head, 1996) as not adjusting to a 'proper' femininity, the apparently strong position of the girls discussed here appears to be related to their skills in traditional male sports. They take pride in and make use of their interests and prowess in sports and describe themselves as very competitive. The girls say that they compete with each other but also with the popular boys, both for overall achievement and good marks, and for doing well during PE lessons. They assert themselves quite successfully against the boys in PE, an otherwise male dominated arena (e.g. Carli, 2004). The girls are active footballers in the local team, and this is deemed to add to their status as well as to influence their relationships to others:

> Pia: Well, most of those who play football or do sports have a lot of friends. They meet and join a lot of friends and then they become popular.
>
> Susan: Most people who are pushy on the football field are also pushy in other ways. You act as a person the same way you would in the field.

The status of football is emphasised in other ways too. Pia's father is well known in the community as a former star in the local football club and the present coach for the grammar school boys. So, as Susan puts it, 'All boys in upper secondary school who are interested in football know who Pia is'. Pia herself seems to enjoy being famous, which of course adds to her own as well as her friends' prestige in school.

Celebrating male relationships

Although these girls are successful both in the formal and the informal arenas of school they seem inclined to celebrate boys and their relations and activities. This brings some ambivalence to their own success:

> A-S: Is it the same or different being with girls as it is with boys?
>
> Pia: Boys are more troublesome.
>
> Susan: Yes, it's more fun being with them.
>
> A-S: In what way?
>
> Susan: Being with girls, an evening for example, we mostly just sit and talk, but when you are hanging about with boys things like happen. They always make up something odd and fun, you know. [Laughing]
>
> [...]

Kim Ling: Perhaps boys are more playful than girls.

Pia: ...and more childish.

Susan: Girls are somewhat; 'No, I can't do that. What will others think?' Boys don't bother that much, I think.

[...]

Pia: We [girls] often exaggerate problems. A small thing may annoy us for a long time and we create huge problems out of it. Boys usually don't bother about things that way.

Susan: Exactly. Girls have to analyse everything in detail before they can leave things behind. Boys treat problems more easily; 'Is it OK with you? Is it OK with me? Okay, let's go then!'

The three girls have been performing successfully in an arena traditionally thought of as male. But despite this and their ownership of most of the valuable features mentioned by others as important, they tend to deprecate girls and girls' activities. They describe girls in general as being duller, more cautious, complicated and not letting go of things. What might be seen as challenging traditional gender stereotypes in fact goes along with a celebration of male activities and relations that might well strengthen traditional gender order.

The immigrant boys
The urban class (7 girl and 11 boys) can be described as silent and 'closed'. As one teacher puts it: 'The pupils don't give much of themselves.'

Being the Other
Ali, Yamal and Hamid are three immigrant boys in the urban class. They do not share the same ethnic background nor the same mother tongue, but they do share the experience of being categorised as immigrants. This knits them tightly together. As seen among the young men interviewed by Sernhede (in press) 'immigrant' might be claimed as a unifying concept. In the present study, ethnicity is strongly related to the peer groupings in the class and in some situations seems more important than gender for social relations. This shows in the case of Zamira, the only immigrant girl in the class. The boys often notice her being lonely and excluded by the other girls

and jointly take care of her. They chat with her, sit next to her in the classroom, let her join their team-work etc. Zamira herself expresses her pleasure that the boys are, as she says, 'like brothers' to her.

The ethnic Swedish pupils in class seem to position the immigrant boys as Others, judging them to 'think in another way than we do' and stating that 'they are different from us'. The ethnic Swedes in class also appear a little afraid of the immigrant boys, who are taller and said to behave in a tougher and noisier manner in class. The immigrant boys, on the other hand, criticise the ethnic Swedish pupils in the class – in particular the boys – for being 'chickens who don't have the guts to speak up for themselves'. They stress the importance of having the courage to stand up for oneself and one's opinions – qualities they largely associate with their own immigrant background.

Developing a pro-school identity

In the interviews the boys report that their attitudes towards schooling have changed dramatically in recent years. From a previous here and now orientation rejecting both academic work and authority, they seem to have developed a more pro-school pupil identity with a future-directed orientation. Ali and Hamid describe the change like this:

> Hamid: Both of us have been engaged in pranks and mischief and messed around with these guys. But now we have put an end to it. Now we are sensible. We have matured and are more concerned about school now.

> Ali: I was hanging around with these guys [in Tengsta] before, but then I started to reconsider things. My parents told me; 'Think about school! Now, you are having fun with your friends and don't care about school, soon enough, in a couple of years, you'll be sitting there with a bad future, living on social welfare... nothing. So be something, something good, then you'll be enjoying life in the future.' So I listened to my parents and thought their advice was a better choice for me.

> A-S: When did you reconsider?

> Hamid: In grade 9.

> Ali: In grade 9. You can ask all the teachers, everybody in school about us, how we behaved when we started grade 7. We turned all the teachers' hair grey. We really behaved like animals if you know what I mean? But now we have calmed down. But earlier, you can ask anyone, everybody had a bad picture of us then, but now we are improving that image.

The boys' new pro-school identity seems also to mean that they have less to do with their former friends in the neighbourhood. They talk about the tough language and pressure in the gang and describe the suburban climate as very destructive and leading to failures and criminality. The boys now stress the importance of the family (cf Sernhede, 2002; Ålund, 1997) and describe their efforts in school as an opportunity to 'pay back' their parents.

> Hamid: You know, our parents are the most important persons to us, they come first. Imagine, they have raised us and they have left their countries for our sake. That's impressive. To think, your parents have come to Sweden to give you a chance to get a good education and to be something... If you fail, your parents of course will be disappointed in you and you'll be disappointed in yourself as well.

The boys say that they rarely hang about with ethnic Swedes after school, although they would like to. They believe that being with Swedish friends would be pleasurable and at the same time good for their language skills. Ali almost glorifies his Swedish classmates, saying: 'Today I realise that Swedish friends might almost be better than immigrant ones'.

The boys emphasise their recent development and explain the changes as due to maturity and responsibility. They have high aspirations for their future career, planning to go on to further education and eventually to obtain jobs such as engineer, dentist or doctor. When asked whether they spend time on schoolwork, Yamal answers 'Of course! I have to do well in the future. It's all about swotting now'. Hamid says his goal is to manage the national tests and improve his grades in mathematics. He is well aware that he needs to work really hard, since he 'wasted' his time in previous years: 'I have lost five years because I was hanging about with the wrong people and didn't care about school.' A teacher confirms the boys' school ambitions, saying: 'They are fixated on the grades'.

According to classroom observations, the boys are quite talkative and demanding of support and help from the teachers. But their forthcoming behaviour evokes mostly positive responses from teachers. The teachers regard the class as colourless and harmless so they see the immigrant boys as a breath of fresh air. As one puts it: 'It would have been boring in the classroom without them'. This re-action differs from other school research which finds that boys from minority ethnic backgrounds are generally viewed as problematic and often described in terms of their deficits (see Gitz-Johansen, 2003).

When talking about popularity, the boys stress the importance of being visible. Hamid describes two different ways of making oneself visible:

> Hamid: Being a nuisance! A tiresome person who doesn't care a damn about school and doesn't care a damn about everything. Who is cruel, tough and knocks everybody down. Then you, sort of, show up yourself. But other persons can be visible in a good way. Like, there are some pupils who are visible because they are nice and kind and at the same time like strong and brave. But they hide that part and just show the nice part. But everybody knows that you shouldn't give that guy any trouble...

Hamid says he does not want to be involved with the tough guys at school or give the impression of being dangerous. In parallel with his shift to pro-school development, he seems to have reformulated his views of ideal masculinities. He says he still can be 'strong and brave', but now in a positive way, which means being humble and school directed. Although Hamid and his friends are distancing themselves from their former 'bad' behaviour, they seem to utilise that be-haviour when constructing their new mature identities. Since they have already proved their tough masculinity, they run less risk of being seen by their peers as soft.

Changed understandings of discrimination
In tandem with their recent orientation to pro-school attitudes, the boys expressed a changed understanding of racism and harsh

treatments in school. Contrary to their former demarcation of 'us against them', they now express more open-minded attitudes to Swedish society and to their teachers and ethnic Swedish schoolmates.

> Hamid: If I may say, in school almost everyone is fairly treated. Almost everyone.
>
> A-S: Who do you think is not fairly treated?
>
> Hamid: Well, there are immigrants that will be treated unfairly.
>
> Ali: Yes, but to be honest – the reasons why they are treated unfairly is not because of their immigrant background. They are treated that way because they are stupid and bad behaving. They are mean to teachers! Then the teachers think... well you know.

This attitude seems to permit them to accept treatment they might not have accepted before. Ali says he is discriminated against by a woman teacher who acts offensively and 'points him out' in front of the class. But Ali has decided not to make a fuss about it, since it is not worth risking his grades and he will soon finish school anyway. Ali also distrusts the teacher Henry, whom he considers too influenced by western thought when teaching. Henry, on the other hand, maintains that he teaches in accordance with the national curriculum. He also says that he prefers to discuss the Middle East issue in class when Ali is absent, because he becomes troublesome. So Henry takes the chance to teach about the foundation of the state of Israel in the very lesson during which Ali was being interviewed. Ali says that this means that his version of history will not be heard in class.

After their previous expectations of racism from their classmates, the boys nowadays demonstrate more acceptance of such tendencies and reformulate them as insignificant. They use various strategies to excuse or play down racist remarks or behaviour in school. One strategy is to attribute discrimination to the individual rather than acknowledge the structural level; another is to grit their teeth and not care – or pretend not to care.

Conclusion

This chapter looked at two groups that seem to manage school successfully. One is a group of girls whose prominent position seems closely related to their interest and prowess in traditionally male sports. They spend time with the popular boys in their class; a kind of networking they believe helps them to speak their mind in class. Whereas previous research mostly shows girls' position in class to be closely related to their informal female networks, this study shows girls also benefiting from associating with boys. Relationships between girls and boys in the top set seem especially to confirm their mutual success on the heterosexual market and thus to establish highly valued femininities and masculinities.

Emergent femininities among the top set girls can be compared to the 'New Girl' in Nordic research who appears both self-confident and academically well integrated (Öhrn, 2000). And these girls compete in a traditional male arena of sports. Physical prowess is strongly associated in schools with hegemonic masculinity. Physical education is a strongly gendered school subject that provides status to those with certain bodily features and behaviours. The top set girls position themselves within traditionally male sports that they celebrate and admire. This seems to go with deprecating traditional female activities. These girls appear very successful but they nevertheless position themselves as subordinated. Although they describe their friendship with girls as valuable and important to their self-confidence and welfare, they consider girls complicated and celebrate boys' more easygoing and joyful way of interacting, as well as their skills in sports. Thus they seem to strengthen the position of traditionally male competences, behaviours and relationships. Male activities help to further these girls' prominent position in school, but also to position them as secondary to boys.

The group of immigrant boys describe a kind of success journey towards pro-school identities that seems largely to rest on their previous experiences and reputation as troublemakers. This background makes it possible for them to subscribe to values of achievement and schooling without being relegated by their friends to the inferior positions of swots. They seem to develop a masculinity that embraces both the strength and danger of their earlier days and the mature responsibility of the young men they are to become. Their change is portrayed as development and maturity, and a way to pay their parents back for what they have given up for them, rather than a wish to accommodate to school expectations or demands. Furthermore, they appear at least partly to escape the teachers' stereotyped images of immigrant boys evident in previous research. Their attempts to succeed in school might be framed in terms of maturity. Thus they could be recognised as conforming to general male – rather than immigrant male – behaviour.

While building on their previous anti-school identities, the boys also emphasise their changed position vis-à-vis the norms prevailing in their local immigrant neighbourhood. Their success implies that they have distanced themselves from the kind of actions and relationships prevailing in this community. While remaining critical of culturalist understandings among teachers and peers in school, they appear to revise their earlier analyses of ethnicity as central to their position. What they once saw as racism when analysing school is now framed partly as individual responsibility, calling attention to the immigrant pupils' own behaviour. They appear to have retreated from their earlier analysis of ethnicity as central to social positions. Like the strong girls, these boys tend to celebrate 'Swedish' male activities and to distance themselves from their own group.

Acknowledgement

A longer version of this article with the same title will appear in Carlson, Marie, Gök, Fatma and Rabo, Annika (Eds): *Reflections on Education in 'Multicultural' Societies. Turkish and Swedish Perspectives.* Swedish Research Institute in Istanbul. The article reports from the project *Young people's perspectives on their schooling. Emergent femininities and masculinities.* The project is part of a large Swedish research programme *Changing Sex/Gender Orders in Schools and Education. Policy, Perspectives and Practice* (GPPP), involving collaboration between educational researchers in Borås University College, Göteborg University, Malmö University College and Umeå University, Sweden.

8

Mixed race women's perspectives on identity: the interplay between postmodernism, essentialism and individualism

Indra Dewan
is a lecturer in Sociology at the University
of East London

Introduction

This chapter describes the constructions of identity and education drawn from interviews with women of mixed heritage in further education colleges in Inner London. The relationship between mixed race identity and post-compulsory education is surprisingly under-researched given the prevalence of people of mixed heritage in Europe and in further education in Britain today, especially in cities such as London which has a significant immigrant population. The women in the study all self-identified as mixed race, and lived and studied in multi-ethnic, traditionally working-class areas of London. The research shows that competing discourses around identity and education were at work in these constructions – the self as to some extent versatile, which is in keeping with the popular postmodernist theory of identity; the self bound by fixed racial categories, heritages, and experiences of discrimination; and the self constructed in individualist terms, especially within the context of education. So although feminist theory may be useful in developing concepts and strategies to combat inequality, its practical application is limited in relation to mixed heritage women. The chapter considers what potential for change can exist in the current climate of diversity, individualism, and depoliticisation, a moment in which even the subaltern is not politicised.

Postmodernist theory and mixed race identity

Traditionally, people of mixed heritage have been seen in terms of pathology, as racial scapegoats, as marginal, 'out of place', and confused about racial identity (Root, 1996; Ifekwunigwe, 1999). Theories of postmodernism have enabled better understanding of mixed heritage people's personal accounts of their experiences (Anzaldua, 1987; Ahmed, 1997; Ifekwunigwe, 1999; Mahtani, 2002), and provided a framework for challenging the view that mixed heritage identity is inherently problematic or pathological. New ways of thinking around identity as socially constructed, fragmented, multiple and shifting have also challenged the view that mixed heritage people belong to a single category such as 'black' or 'Indian', and have allowed them to define themselves in heterogeneous, as opposed to mono-racial, ways.

The introduction of a 'mixed race' category in the 2001 census in Britain formally endorsed the individual's right to self-identify as mixed race: mixed heritage people no longer need to choose between distinct mono-racial categories, for example, identify as *either* black *or* white, but can identify in dual-racial terms, i.e. as *both* black *and* white. Aspinall (2003) has argued that the 2001 census categories have mistakenly focused on race rather than ethnic and cultural identifications, thereby reinforcing the rigidity of racial boundaries (289), and urges new ways of thinking which allow for 'hybridised identities that represent allegiances to multiple groups rather than an outcome from two putatively 'pure' categories' (292).

As the number of people of mixed heritage has increased in Britain, attention has also increasingly focused on them as harbingers of a more egalitarian, progressive and multicultural society. In fact, one might argue that they are viewed as *epitomising* the postmodern subject. As possessors of two cultures at least, they are celebrated as cultural bridge-builders who have the potential to cure society of its racial ills. This is symptomatic of the current tendency in public discourse to replace race discourse with culture discourse. As Frankenberg (1993) has pointed out, cultural difference is seen as harmless and enriching, whereas racial difference is not. Mahtani (2002) has described the celebration of mixed race diversity thus:

> It has also been assumed that the 'mixed race' individual has the solution for the world's racist problems in a vacant celebration of sanitised cultural hybridity, where the mixed race person is seen as a 'rainbow child' glimmering with hope for a colour-blind future. (470-471)

The BBC internet site provides insight into popular assumptions around mixed heritage people in Britain. The opening article of Race UK, entitled *The changing face of Britain: Britain's blurring ethnic mix*, is a good example of what Parker and Song (2001) have called the 'celebration' discourse of mixed race people as 'embodiments of the progressive and harmonious intermingling of cultures and people' and 'exemplars of contemporary cultural creativity' (2001, 4). The leading caption, flanked by a photo of Dawn French and Lenny Henry, triumphantly claims: 'The United Kingdom has one of the fastest growing mixed race populations in the world, fuelled by the continuing rise of inter-ethnic relationships'.

The article goes on to claim that 'Britons of all shades are embracing each other more than ever before', and informs us that celebrities such as Michael Caine and Trevor Macdonald, Sade and Salman Rushdie are, or have been, in mixed race relationships. Shirley Bassey, Oona King MP and Hanif Kureshi moreover, are 'high-profile examples of Britain's burgeoning mixed race population'. Inter-racial liaisons are described as thriving: 'inter-racial relationships were flourishing, with a fifth of Asian men and 10 per cent of Asian women opting for a white partner'. The purpose of this article appears to be to demonstrate the liberalism and open-mindedness of British society. Yet it has racist undertones in that it focuses on the superficial and urbane, and exoticises mixed race identity and relationships.

Limited versatility: the postmodernist findings

In the next three sections I discuss the interview data in relation to theories of postmodernism, essentialism and individualism. My basic premise is that knowledge is historically and culturally specific and that identities are socially constructed through language (e.g. Foucault, 1972, 1979). I reject essentialism as a theory and look to the role of discourse in constructing social phenomena and ideas. Respondents' references to essentialist, individualist or post-modernist notions of self should therefore be understood within the context of the discourses which form their identities. The words presented here are not representative of who the respondents really are or what they really believe, but are articulations which reflect their own versions of reality at a given moment.

In contrast to the commonly held view that people with mixed heritages epitomise the postmodern subject, the women in this study saw themselves neither as an amalgam of many different selves, nor as 'free-floating' entities in the postmodern sense. Whilst welcoming diversity and embracing an 'anything goes' notion of mixed race personhood, they largely made sense of their everyday lives through the lens of race. Discourses around race were intrinsic to the women's sense of who they were and also to their experiences of categorisation, exclusion and discrimination.

Articulations around mixed race identity were representative of the postmodernist position insofar as they advocated the *idea* of self-definition and the freedom to self-define. Many respondents evoked a diversity discourse of mixed race, rendering concepts of race, appearance, culture, nationality, religion, etc. as synonymous with each other. The following quote illustrates this position.

> [Mixed race means]... coming from two different races. Mediterranean – Spain, Greece, Turkey – is a race separate from European. Part of what comes into your race is your religion, like Pakistani and Indian are different races. Cypriot-Turks and Cypriot-Greeks consider themselves different from mainland Turks or Greeks – they speak each other's language, and the traditions are identical, but a Greek is a Greek and a Turk is a Turk. I can tell Greeks and Turks apart. Germans and English are a different race because they look different – I can tell a German a mile away. Soraya (English/Turkish)

The postmodernist theory of identity and the idea that mixed heritage people are bridge-builders between today's imperfect world and a better future was also supported by the respondents' views on difference. Although most respondents said that they saw being different as a disadvantage, many also saw other people's curiosity about them as a positive thing in that it provided the potential for greater understanding between people generally. Being able to adapt to different racial and cultural settings was also seen as a positive thing by some respondents, as Corinne (Jamaican/Irish) pointed out said:

> I can get on with anybody. At home I live in a white culture, and then at my father's house I'm living around a black culture, so I'm seeing two worlds, two cultures, two sets of people... so I know how to get along with white people very well and I know how to get along with black people very well, so I think it's broadened my mind to just getting along with people as a whole. Corinne (Jamaican/Irish)

The significance of race: the essentialist findings

The women drew on essentialist notions of race and selfhood in various ways. Race was not an unpalatable or unnameable aspect of life, as much literature and public discourse would have us believe, but was intrinsic to the women's self-perceptions and to their experiences of categorisation, exclusion and discrimination.

First, many of the women emphatically rejected the concept of race, and stated that race and colour were not important in how they defined themselves. In response to the question 'How do you define yourself?' Adriana and Anabel said:

> Not by the colour of my skin at all, never, how I am, how I present myself, how I interact with other people. It's a matter of common sense, not looking at someone, like they say, not looking at the book and judging it by the cover. Adriana (Angolan/Portuguese)

> As a human being. Personally I dislike it when people say I'm black, because I will tell them if you look at my bag, that's black, I'm not black. To be honest, I'm not too keen about this issue of race and colour, I just view myself as a professional woman... one who is capable of functioning at a very high level of competence. Anabel (Guyanese/Indian-White)

Second, whilst rejecting formal classifications of race based on features which distinguished people as 'raced', many respondents also said that being mixed race was important to them. As such, they made use of the concept of race in seemingly paradoxical ways.

Related to this is the third point. Almost all the women in the study felt that they were wrongly perceived and categorised by others in mono-racial terms, that is to say, some felt they were seen as black, a few as white, and some as belonging to a racial or cultural category which was totally unconnected with their own perceptions of self-hood. For example, one respondent who described herself as Burmese-Welsh said she was seen as Chinese; a Colombian/Jewish-Polish woman said people usually thought that she was Indian or Pakistani. This suggests that, despite the prevalence of mixed heritage people and a dominant postmodern discourse of identity, the discourse of mono-racialism still predominates. One might argue that self-assertions of mixed race were in fact made in defiance of monoracial categorisation, as in: I am me, I am *mixed race*, not all those other things you might think I am.

Fourth, self-identification as mixed race was expressed as an assertion of both parents' racial heritages, where these heritages were seen as literally constituting respondents' identities. Many respondents were precise about their exact racial mix – traced back to parents, grand-parents, and great grand-parents – even where the father was absent or marginal in the respondent's life, and regardless of whether the respondent was brought up in a white or black household. In fact, two-thirds of the respondents were brought up in one-parent households, usually with the mother; only in two cases was the mother absent or marginal. Lianne said:

> When people bring it up I have to make sure they know I'm black and white. If people say 'are you black?' I say no, I'm both, my mum's in the picture. I feel mixed race because of the colour of my skin, that's the main reason. And because of my father. I've got to admit he's still there – he brought me into this world, so I can't just say I'm white, I couldn't do that, I don't think it would be right, denying part of my family. Lianne (St. Lucian/English)

Similarly, Petra said:

> Because that's where my mum's from and I'm part of my mum...it's important, and you know you're from there so you got to take an insight into what kind of things they do. You can't forget about something that is part of you. Petra (Portuguese/Black African)

A few respondents talked in depth about identity transitions in which they reclaimed the 'half' of their identity which had previously been denied or lain dormant. This retrieval invariably involved an assertion of their mixed race identity where this was 'who they really are.' The denied and reclaimed 'half' was always the father's heritage, which in every case was also the minority heritage.

Aisha had always been made to feel different and a misfit:

> My father's relatives came to stay and there were always questions about my name and why I looked different, and religion-wise too... Being half Indian I was different and people couldn't figure out what it was – they thought I must be Italian, that's as exotic as they could think.

Aisha talked about two main turning points in her life, in which she first rejected her racial and cultural heritage and invented herself as white, and then later accepted her mixed race heritage. The first turning point at the age of nine involved a rejection of her father, and the realisation that she could fight back against being seen as Indian by simply refusing everything Indian:

> It had built up and at that age I realised that I could actually do things that could enable me to reject it, I didn't just have to be upset about those things, but I could say well I've got a second name I can use, I don't have to eat this food, I can tell people my father is the neighbour, I can make up stories, I don't have to be this person. I went by my middle name which is Christine, because Aisha was too foreign, because I didn't want people to know who my father was, I didn't want to have anything to do with anything that was Indian. Aisha (Indian/White American)

Aisha recalls her second turning point when she was 14 or 15, when she began meeting new people outside school and started using the name Aisha again. She believed that, despite the questions and taunts directed at her as a child and teenager, she must have been getting some positive signals about her difference and the way she looked, and this helped her to see that being part-Indian was 'alright, and even a good thing', and that it was 'maybe an advantage to look a bit different, not to look like every blond blue-eyed person around you.'

The fifth point which shows how powerful a discourse race was in the articulations of the women was how some respondents defined themselves in relation to homogeneously perceived others, and drew on essentialist notions of blackness and whiteness in which a person's attitude or way of behaving was linked to the biological fact of their race. Essentialism is described by Burr as

> a way of understanding the world that sees things (including human beings) as having their own particular essence or nature, something which can be said to belong to them and which explains how they behave...(1995:19)

Keisha, who described herself as 'fully mixed', distinguished between the supposed difference in the personalities of black and white girls, and recognised and rejected what she saw as the negative 'black' personality traits in herself and other black people. She chose not to associate with black girls because of their discriminatory attitudes towards white people, nor with white girls because of their 'barbie-ness', opting for a racially mixed group of boys who just had fun. It is important to stress that these articulations were made at a particular moment and do not necessarily indicate that Keisha made these race/personality/behaviour links more generally. However, communications on the subject of race and behaviour may also reflect the idea which lies at the heart of racism: that there are natural links between race and behaviour. Keisha said:

> To be honest I hardly ever hang around with black girls cos there's something, I just don't like their attitude. I do have a temper and everything, but certain things they do I don't agree, like most things they do I don't like, their racist comments about white people or mixed people and that. The white girls I hang around with have been called things you wouldn't like to hear, and they know what it's like. It's their personality, it's about personality – some white girls I won't hang around with because it's too like a Barbie, too much like a Barbie, so I'm like you're not my type of person. Like it

depends on the person itself. Black girls I'd call more like a tomboy, more like a tomboy than a Barbie. Keisha ('Fully Mixed')

For Keisha, the gender-specific racial diversity of such a group, in which everyone except girls was understood to be the same regardless of race or colour, formed a protection against racism. She said:

It's like when I go out with a group of them it has to be mixed. So you know when you're in a group and someone passes a racist comment, it affects all of us not just one, cos in a way we're all different, and it's not about your culture.

Keisha made a distinction between gender difference and all other kinds of difference. Whereas being mixed and different had positive and transformative potential insofar as it could ultimately challenge racism, difference and the transgression of norms of gendered behaviour were seen as problematic. Thus the group was gender-exclusive: Keisha simply distanced herself from what she saw as negative female traits, and aligned herself firmly with the boys. She created a tomboy/Barbie dualism in her description of the difference between black girls and white – white girls displayed more feminine traits insofar as Barbie represents the archetypal feminine woman – whereas black girls expressed themselves in more tomboyish and therefore more masculine ways. This perceived masculinity in black girls was associated with, as Keisha said, a type of 'personality', 'attitude', 'temper', and 'racist comments', yet Keisha did not represent the boys as expressing these characteristics. Keisha appears to have framed herself within a specific version of femininity which rejects what she saw as female expressions of masculinity or excessive femininity.

Sixth, 'incorrectly' categorised as black yet self-identifying as mixed race caused problems for some respondents insofar as they were seen as neither white enough by white people nor as black enough by black people, so experienced discrimination from both black people and white. Cathrina expressed a sense of resignation, claiming that there has been little progress in suturing racial divisions. She said:

Yeah, like some black people yeah, think like, cos you know back in the day it used to be like blacks on one side and whites on the other, a lot of racism used to be going on. Like I was on the bus and I heard someone say that, ah, mixed race people they shouldn't be made, black people should stay with black people and white people should stay with white people. Like when you listen to [names music band], some black people think that half-caste people shouldn't listen to it, cos they got a part of white inside. Cathrina (Jamaican/Irish)

Lindsey expressed her anger at black people for denying her mixed heritage. She said:

It's mainly young black people talking about white people. They come out with rubbish and say 'no offence', that really bugs me. I have to defend my whiteness in those situations. Sometimes I have to say like, excuse me, my mum's white you know, and they'll say but I'm not talking about your mum, something stupid like that, they just don't get the point. People like that I can't be bothered to explain myself to. Lindsey (Bajan/Scottish)

Aleasha talked about what she saw as the problem of cultural separatism in her class, where black people tended to stay on one side of the room and white people on the other. Her experience was of 'constantly being bullied' and ostracised for 'acting too white'. She said:

Black people won't talk to you if you show knowledge or intel-ligence. The other day I was talking to a boy and he was like: you're so white, you act like white people, and I'm like: just because you see an intelligent black person in front of you that means they're acting white? I'm like, to be black and to be intelligent that means you're trying to act white? Aleasha (Grenadian-Scottish/ Dominican)

To sum up so far, most of the respondents did not accept racial designations, rejected the concept of race, and at the same time felt they were perceived by others in racially designated ways. This corresponds with post-structuralist theory insofar as respondents felt their identities were to some extent determined by other people's positioning. At the same time, the women drew on race discourse to define themselves, where these self-identifications usually endorsed parents' racial heritages, and were sometimes invoked in opposition to racially homogeneous 'others' such as black people. It could be argued that race as a means of self-definition – as opposed to race as a means of categorisation – was a powerful aspect of respondents' identities precisely because of the denial of their dual or multiple racial identities. Self-definition as mixed race may therefore be understood as an act of separation from, defence against, or indeed subversion of the rigid boundaries of racial homogenisation imposed from outside.

Mixed race as an aspect of personality: the 'individualist' findings

Many respondents appeared to have no difficulty in separating self-definition as mixed race from race as a concept or external phenomenon. In several respondents' articulations around selfhood, an easy alignment between mixed race identity and personality was also present. The assertion 'I am just me' was juxtaposed with 'I am mixed race'. Whilst appearance, usually focusing on hair and skin colour, was frequently mentioned, respondents were anxious to put across that their identities were not based on the superficial designations of race or colour but on what 'lay beneath' their skin. Respondents wanted to be seen by others as unique individuals, where being valued as mixed race was intrinsic to that uniqueness.

The discourse of individualism was most obviously drawn upon in the women's articulations around education. In stark contrast to the salience of race in the findings on identity, explicit references to race were dropped altogether in discussions about education. The respondents' position on race was therefore ambivalent: within the broader context of their everyday experiences, many respondents felt excluded and discriminated against by others, but within the context of education, race was not perceived as a marker of disadvantage, and was seen as irrelevant to the educational choices and opportunities available to people. The mass availability of education was in itself a marker of an equal society and most respondents saw their own lives as testimonies to the success of government initiatives which aimed to provide greater equality of opportunity in education. The principal idea expressed by the respondents was that in being responsible individuals able to make autonomous decisions within an egalitarian system of governance, people were ultimately responsible for their own success or failure (see Beck *et al*, 2001; Colley *et al*, 2001).

115

The onus of responsibility for society's ills thus falls back onto the individual. Inequalities are not seen as the responsibility of government. At the same time, the perceived irrelevance of race is symptomatic of what might be referred to as 'colour-blindness' about the reality of race (Ahmed, 1997, Tessman, 1999), in which the effects of racialisation are maintained precisely through race invisibility. Race, in other words, is deconstructed to the extent that it vanishes altogether, and the power differential therefore also disappears. One could argue therefore that *any* differences between people, not just those concerning power imbalances, but also those relating to achievement and failure in education, may be inadvertently directed back onto the person, rather than being attributed to the unequal effects of power relationships.

The research demonstrates that competing discourses were at work. Whilst the findings support the postmodernist theory of identity insofar as mixed race personhood was constructed by the women as pluralistic and to some extent versatile, respondents did not see identities as *fundamentally* dynamic in the postmodern sense. The findings, moreover, also challenge essentialist theory which has traditionally classified identity in mono-racial and mono-cultural terms. An essentialist model which incorporates dual or multiple aspects may therefore be more apt for contextualising the respondents' mixed race identities. Root's (1992) assertion that mixed race identities are grounded in duality and multiplicity in that they are socially ambiguous and fluid, and yet are contained within typified racial boundaries, is useful for understanding this double position.

One of the main theoretical challenges which these findings pose is how to reconcile 'raced' and 'individualist' notions of self. In a conference paper, Skinner (2004) discusses how contemporary biology such as DNA testing is being linked to new notions of 'who we really are', and that biologism is reopening old debates about sameness and difference and providing people with new ways of experiencing and talking about identity. In this context, I would argue that the assertion 'I am just me, I am mixed race' need not be understood as a purely individualistic articulation but may show how perceptions of biological heritage can be felt to be a powerful and unique part of the individual. The findings show that not only were elements of postmodernism and essentialism combined, but essentialist and individualist aspects of personhood were integrated in the respondents' constructions of self.

The concept of race as a social construction is not disputed. The dominance of race, and the persistence of categorisation, and of discriminatory attitudes and practices in the lives of the respondents, however, indicate a need to retain the concept of race. The research also indicates that there is an unequivocal need to investigate further the meaning of race in mixed race people's lives and within social discourse. Whilst understanding that the notion of race is a product of discourse without inherent meaning in itself, it is only through the meanings ascribed to this term that sense can be made of the respondents' articulations about race.

Race and the feminist political agenda

The study indicates that some form of political intervention is needed to overcome the different forms of discrimination experienced by mixed heritage women in their daily lives. From a feminist perspective, individuals must organise collectively, re-essentialise so to speak, for an emancipatory antiracist project to develop. The question of individual rights for mixed heritage people and the discovery of new forms of identification have been the impetus behind their official British recognition through the new 'mixed race' category in the 2001 census. One of the key questions this has opened up in critical mixed race theory has been 'who counts as mixed race?' This parallels the debate within the black feminist movement about 'who counts as black?' and is intrinsic to this debate insofar as whoever counts as mixed race cannot also count as black. Therefore the main challenge against a mixed race category has been that to accept such a category would weaken the struggle against racism, rather than create the possibility for struggle against it (Gordon, 1995) because many of those who previously defined as black would defect to a mixed race grouping.

This modernist position has been criticised for being a universalistic conception of personhood which results in exclusion and derision (Anthias and Yuval-Davis, 1992).

The modernist perspective, moreover, is difficult to sustain within the current climate of individualism. It appears to undermine the possibility of collective political action in that power relations are created within discourses which prevent the development of the political subject. Whilst some individual respondents may have re-garded themselves as political, neither a collective identity nor political or social reform appeared to be pressing issues for most of them. This was shown in a number of ways. Only one respondent identified as politically black, and nobody explicitly referred to their mixed race identity as a political identity. Although essentialist dis-course was drawn upon in constructions of identity, there was no evidence of a desire for a fixed mixed race category. Furthermore, respondents bought into the discourse of meritocracy, especially within the context of education, and felt that they were equal to everyone else. Moreover, they either did not believe that structural inequalities existed, or assumed that any inequalities which did exist were the problem and responsibility of people themselves, rather than a problem of structure and resources which should be solved by government. Even amongst the few respondents who were re-flexive about issues of inequality, responsibility was ultimately to the 'self', and not to a collective 'other'.

These factors inevitably have implications for a feminist eman-cipatory politics. Where people do not feel implicated in power re-lations – as is evident in this study – and regard themselves as inno-cent by-standers, they cannot be politically motivated, and the possibility for emancipatory action becomes blocked or limited. The respondents' assertions of their own heterogeneity, and resistance to what they saw as homogeneity, can be described as an anti-poli-tical stance. Conversely, the respondents' self-identifications in specifically raced terms were in themselves individual political acts, and acts of resistance to the idea that we all live happily together in a benign culturally diverse society. The most explicit political aspect of respondents' articulations, however, appeared to be the distinc-tion they made between daily experiences of race difference, stereo-typing, categorisation and discrimination, and a more promising future in which the negative effects of race did not exist, and where the very presence of people of mixed heritage would contribute to overcoming such prejudices and inequities in society. Perhaps, then, the respondents saw themselves as to some extent individually and personally implicated in making the world a better place.

9

Self-identification and ethnicity: 'You can't be an *English* Pakistani'

Chris Gaine

Professor of Applied Social Policy at the
University of Chichester, England

Introduction

The most recent census (2001) revealed that 7.9 per cent of Britain's population are from visible minority ethnic groups – that is to say, people identifiable by skin colour – with about 1.5 per cent from 'white' minority groups. Despite some newer immigration and the growth of a mixed population, the settled migrant groups of the 1950s and their descendants are still the largest. The evolving picture raises questions about identity, self-definition and belonging with which schools must engage.

This research analyses a unique set of data relating to ethnic self-identification amongst British young people. The antiracist website www.britkid.org is a resource designed for school and individual use that explores aspects of ethnicity, identity and belonging. While originally aimed at a white majority audience, it is also encountered by minority ethnic young people and this provided an opportunity to gain some insight into how they saw themselves. Forty thousand users were asked to self-identify in terms of ethnicity and religion, potentially generating a large source of data on these aspects of identity. As a data source it provides some challenges in terms of reliability and validity, but it nevertheless offers unique insight into the salience and overlap in young people's consciousness of categories such as race, ethnicity, nationality and religion.

Asking the questions

The website was written with younger adolescents as the main target audience, intended mainly for use in schools as well as by individuals at home. The site went on line late in 1998. There are no ethical difficulties in using this data since it is entirely anonymous, with no access to the server that might provide a route to users' computer addresses. Though not obligatory, the opening page of the site asked the users to fill in basic personal data, including:

How old are you?	[ ]
Are you a boy or a girl?	boy ☐ girl ☐
How would you describe your ethnic origin?	[ ]
What would you say your religion was?	[ ]

The ethnicity question tried to get at users' self-definition without feeding them clues in pre-set categories. This was particularly important in trying to discover what kinds of self-description were salient to the young target audience. Had we asked 'what is your race?' most young users would have understood what we meant and arguably we would have accessed their common-sense understanding of the term. We asked 'How would you describe your ethnic origin?' to avoid conferring legitimacy to the term 'race' in an educational context.

Ethnicity

Identifying and defining ethnicity is a contentious issue in Britain and elsewhere. If we are to avoid the essentialising assumptions of racial categories, any definition of ethnicity ought to combine elements of what is in our heads when we distinguish social groups, without going down the road of fixed 'racial' characteristics. It should also involve self-consciousness as a group. Schermerhorn (1970) defines an ethnic group thus:

> ...a collectivity within a larger society, having real or putative ancestry, memories of a shared or historical past, and a cultural focus on one or more symbolic elements defined as the epitome of their people-hood. (p12)

The self-consciousness as a group, the existence of and conscious-ness of the collectivity may be internally generated or may be at least partly imposed from outside. In this vein, Jenkins (2004: 97), citing Barth, suggests that ethnic identities are made up of three elements:

- ascriptions and self-ascriptions held and understood by the social actors involved and thus playing a role in inter-actions
- certain processes that generate collective forms
- boundary maintenance and group recruitment.

Let us examine the element of ascription and boundary main-tenance.

In Britain a key element in this derives from the country's migration history. Since the 1950s the largest groups *perceived* as ethnically dif-ferent have originated from ex-colonies: the Indian sub-continent, the Caribbean, and in smaller numbers, from Africa and Hong Kong. This has led to a broad but widely used three-part ethnic categorisa-tion of 'Asian', 'Black' and 'Chinese', with the following sub-categories:

		2001 Census data	
Asian	Indian	1.8%	
	Pakistani	1.3%	3.6%
	Bangladeshi	0.5%	
Black	Caribbean	1.0%	1.8%
	African	0.8%	
Chinese	Mainly Hong Kong	0.4%	0.4%

The groupings in this table partly reflect geography and culture and partly biological assumptions: in other words it is based partly on physical appearance. But it reflects something else too: physical appearance is correlated with a continuing pattern of discrimination in employment, housing, the criminal justice system and education, a coded, implicit but usually present reference in immigration legislation and explicit reference in race discrimination law. Skin colour and physical appearance, in other words, have been key aspects of 'ethnicisation' as well as racialisation (Reeves, 1983), key signifiers of difference.

This is exemplified in the 2001 British National Census, in which the Office for National Statistics (ONS) tried to count minorities in terms that made sense to the minorities themselves and that resonated with perceptions amongst the sometimes discriminating majority. The terminology is revealing for what it says and does not say. The Census questions open with 'What is your ethnic group?' and then refer to 'cultural background' of which the first option is not cultural at all but biological: 'white'. Other categories blur biology and national roots. The 'mixed' category is largely racial, for instance 'white and Asian', but other categories try to give space to more cultural attributes, though they are named either through geography – 'African' – or nationality – 'Indian'. One has, therefore, both a (social) 'race' and an ethnic group, which at times merge together confusingly. This is not to criticise the ONS: it is simply trying to capture what is in British heads and social practices and this changes over time.

Tariq Modood (1992) provides useful clarification of this with notions of 'mode of being' and 'mode of oppression'. The latter is primarily the crude classification of race, ascribed by others and constituting a key element in social experience, and structuring ways in which people are oppressed. 'Mode of being' is more about self-ascription: the elements of ethnicity that are cultural and about self-consciousness as a group, the features of ethnicity identified by Schermerhorn but also argued by Modood to include 'strategies of self definition, symbolic and real forms of resistance against marginality' (1994: 8).

Ethnic identity is therefore a slippery concept. We might try to capture people's self-categorisations in a census, but we delude ourselves if we think we are capturing something objective and fixed. As Jenkins puts it:

> ...interaction across the boundary is the *sine qua non* of ethnic identity... its persistence or revision is a dialectical process of collective identification, with internal and external moments. Ethnicity is always a two way street, involving 'them' as well as 'us' ... Internal identification and external identification are mutually entangled. (2004: 99)

So 'ethnic group' is not unambiguously and solely a social term. It refers mostly to culture but at times invokes physical appearance as a boundary marker, something that may make sense to those within the group as well as those outside it. All such boundaries are fluid, ethnicity is not fixed, and while there may be some stability in terms of groups, individuals may have a more ambiguous and mobile identity. Modood *et al* observe

> While some groups assert a racial identity based on the experience of having suffered racism, others choose to emphasise their family origins and homeland ... others group around a caste or religious sect ... while yet others promote a trans-ethnic identity like Islam. Yet the competition between identities is not simply a competition between groups; it is within communities and within individuals. It is quite possible for someone to be torn between the claims of being, for example, 'black', Asian, Pakistani and Muslim, of having to choose between them and the solidarities they represent... having to reconcile them with the claims of gender, class and Britishness. (1994:5)

Modood *et al* explored Britishness explicitly in 1997, using ethnic identification in a pairing with being British (see page 126).

For all groups the consciousness and possibility of mixed identity is clear, suggesting they are not incompatible identities. It is noteworthy that more than a quarter of all groups did not see themselves as British. This was related to birthplace in some cases but was also true of British-born respondents.

> ...they found it difficult to call themselves 'British' because they felt that the majority of white people did not accept them as British because of their race or cultural background. (Modood *et al*, 1997: 330)

percentages

'In many ways I see myself as... ' (i) British (ii) respondent's ethnic group

| | Caribbean | | Indian | | Pakistani | | Bangladeshi | | Chinese | |
	British Caribbean		British Indian		British Pakistani		British Bangladeshi		British Chinese	
Agree	64	87	62	91	66	90	60	92	44	94
Disagree	31	9	27	5	23	4	23	5	46	5
Neither	5	4	12	5	12	6	17	3	10	1

Derived from Modood et al, 1997:329

It is highly likely that, had 'English' been substituted for 'British' in the above question, fewer respondents would have identified themselves this way. 'English' seems to be a more exclusive and racialised category, claiming some distinctiveness from the Irish, Welsh and Scots. This is complicated by the assumption amongst the English – one that has long irritated other Britons – that real Britishness is somehow English. The Runnymede Trust's *The Future of Multi-Ethnic Britain* argues

> Britishness, as much as Englishness, has systematic, largely unspoken, racial connotations. Whiteness nowhere features as an explicit condition of being British, but it is widely understood that Englishness, and therefore by extension Britishness, is racially coded. ...[...]... Race is deeply entwined with ... the idea of nation. (Runnymede Trust, 2000: 38)

Certainly both identifications are racially coded, but I was not convinced that they are almost indistinguishable and indeed this proved to be so in my data. ONS data published after the Runnymede study confirms this:

> People from the white British group were more likely to describe their national identity as English, rather than British. However, the opposite was true of the non-white groups, who were far more likely to identify themselves as British. (ONS, cited in the *Guardian* 8/01/2004).

It is worth noting here the extent of public discussion about the ubiquitous display of the *English* flag during the European football tournament in 2004. Commentators were divided about how much this had racial, even racist, overtones and how much such overtones were undermined and neutralised by the number of minorities who flew the flag (not to mention the six black players who played in the team). The flag has been even more widely displayed during the World Cup season of 2006, with rather less discussion about any racialised meaning.

Analysing the data

Cleaning

The scale of the database was formidable, in that there were 39,297 logins, with nine fields corresponding to initial questions but another 25 fields indicating where on the site users had visited. Only the data from *three* of these 34 fields is discussed here.

Because terminology and conceptions of identity differ in different countries, I eliminated entries that appeared to originate outside Britain. This reduced the useable data set to 36,157. Excluding any incomplete logins further reduced this set by 16,512, leaving 19,645.

'Cleaning' the data was particularly laborious because of the huge range of self-descriptions used, let alone the hasty spelling that often featured. The first six data fields of un-cleaned material typically looked like this:

Name	Age	Boy/Girl	Ethnicity	Religion	Country
Elisa	0	g	English	protestant	Uk
sunny	48	g	english	c e	0
susie.c	14	g	white	c of e	England
penny	0	g	caucasian	0	England
snuff	29	b	British	agnostic	England
LinC	15	b	English	Christian	England
angel	14	g	white	RC	england
sa	8	b	english	coe	englanf
donkey	30	g	caucasian	0	Scotland
yasha	51	g	Jewish	none	UK
Lukcas	10	b	British	aetheist	0
saleem	0	b	pakistani	islam	uk

In order to make the data useable, every individual line had to be examined for consistency to determine whether it was reliable enough to use. The most obvious example of a discounted entry was someone who entered their religion as Jewish but their nickname as 'Hitler'. I had various interim categories that resulted in the exclusion of 1376 entries, leaving 18,269 to examine at face value. As part of the line-by-line analysis described above, I wanted to make some judgements about the ages of users. A large number were spurious: those 'over 100' and those under eight were easily discounted, but entries like some of those in the original data example shown above need interpreting. To take two examples:

beth   51   g   Jewish none   UK

I saw no reason not to take this age at face value. Beth is not an unlikely name for someone Jewish to give themselves and the other details are unremarkable. On the other hand

farty   87   g   martian zion   entrail

contains no useable data at all. On this basis I calculated that most users were adolescents between the ages of 11 and 15, although a substantial number of adult entries were not analysed here.

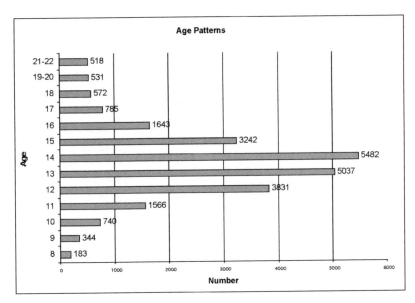

Having reduced the dataset to entries that could be taken seriously, it was still a constant preoccupation that although a good deal of data would be presented in quantitative form, almost every line of the final dataset of 18,269 involved a qualitative judgement. Take as an example someone who described themselves as Scottish but also Sikh: this would almost certainly be someone of Indian descent, stating that they saw themselves as Scottish first rather than 'Asian' or Indian', or indeed 'British'. This can be stated confidently because the Sikh faith does not proselytise and there are virtually no Sikhs in the world who do not have Indian Punjabi roots. On this basis I discarded a person who logged in as white and Sihk (*sic*). This kind of identification and naming of identity was what I was looking at, but what of someone who wrote white and 'Muslim', 'Buddhist' or 'Hindu' instead of Sikh? The Hindu is very likely to have roots outside the UK, but could *possibly* be a white Scottish follower. Islam also seeks to proselytise, so such an entry could be a white Scot.

After doing this extensive qualitative cleaning of the original entries, I sought to look more closely at how people categorised themselves, the words they used to make sense of our question.

Self-ascribed ethnicity: white people

The majority of people (who were obviously white) simply said so (55% of 6635), with the remaining 45 per cent fairly evenly divided between 'British' (2735) and 'English' (2667):

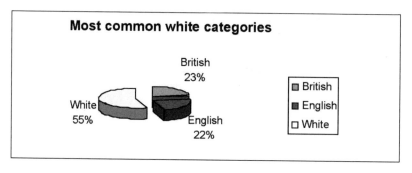

But there were other ways (see chart).

Almost all of these employ a 'racial' characteristic, underlining the significance of colour in common-sense understandings of ethnicity. There is no way of telling their roots, but twelve entries answered the question with 'by my skin colour'.

About 700 specified a British regional identity. It was seldom possible to distinguish between Northern Irish and those from the Republic of Ireland).

Some of those in the graph (on page 132) who describe themselves as Scottish or Welsh could possibly also be black or of mixed heritage. I excluded any who indicated a religion other than Christianity

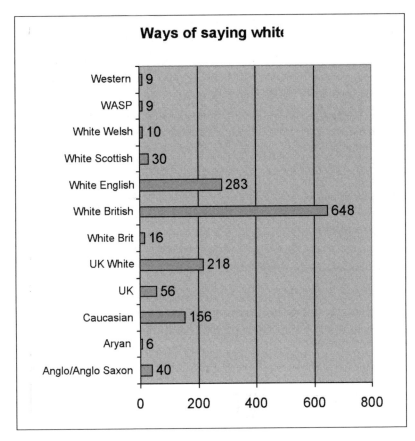

Ways of saying white

Western	9
WASP	9
White Welsh	10
White Scottish	30
White English	283
White British	648
White Brit	16
UK White	218
UK	56
Caucasian	156
Aryan	6
Anglo/Anglo Saxon	40

so as to separate those likely to have roots in the Indian sub-continent, but some people of Caribbean or African descent could still be 'hidden' in the figures. From what I found later under self-ascription I am confident this is a very small number.

Some people of European descent resident in Britain signalled their whiteness with terms such as American/White American, and Australian. For those with roots elsewhere in Europe, a range of very specific descriptions was given. These were almost always by nationality, with the odd exception like 'Slav' or 'Aryan German'.

Self-ascribed ethnicity: black people

The category 'black' generally refers to people of African descent, either directly or via the Caribbean. Here is the wide range of self-descriptions used:

Black British	63	English African	1
Black British Caribbean	8	Scottish African	1
British Caribbean	1	Black African British	1
Black UK	7	Black African Welsh	1
Caribbean UK	1	Black	7
Black English	5	Black other	2
Afro British	1	African Caribbean	42
British West Indian	3	Black Afro Caribbean	1
Afro Caribbean British	2	Black Jamaican	4
English Caribbean	2	Afro Trinidadian	1
English Jamaican	7	Jamaican Barbadian	1
English Barbadian	2	Welsh West Indian	1
Nigerian African	1		
		Total	166

It was surprising that the term 'English' was used at all, even if only twelve entries out of 166 – amounting to 7 per cent. A good deal is written in the UK about acceptable terminology with which to describe or name black people (e.g. Gaine, 2005) and the two most used terms here are those most commentators would recommend.

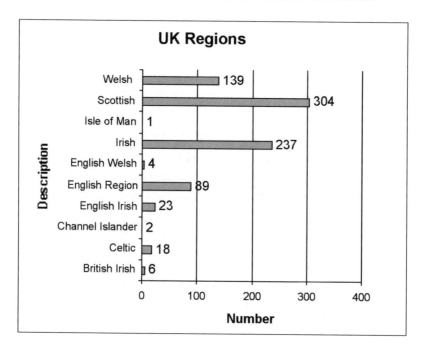

Self-ascribed ethnicity: people of Asian descent

To establish the respondents most likely to have roots in south Asia, entries for religion and ethnic group were compared.

Sikhs are a distinct subgroup of British Asians easy to identify because virtually every Sikh has Indian Punjabi roots. Of the 159 Sikhs who used the site, 66 gave their ethnic group as Indian and 24 as Asian. Four said Punjabi (one further identifying himself by his caste group) and four put Sikh as their ethnic group as well as their religion. Nine said they were British, four said English, and two Welsh. Thirty five made no entry, but only one wrote 'don't know'. A significantly higher percentage (59%) identified themselves as Indian or Asian than that found by Modood (1997). It may be that Sikhs are more likely to do this than Hindus (see chart on page 134) or that a younger population sees the issue differently. The numbers are too small to draw any conclusions, but it would be intriguing if younger Sikhs were less likely than an older sample to see themselves as British.

Of the 946 *Muslims* the largest specifically identifiable groups were, predictably, Pakistanis and Bangladeshis, with the other groups reflecting the diversity of British Muslims. 'Other' included small numbers from Indonesia, China, Algeria, Egypt, Malaysia, Albania and the Caribbean, and twenty white people.

Thirty seven people preferred to see their ethnicity as well as their religion as Islamic, rather than signal any national affiliation. The category 'British etc' (n=62) has some interesting features: three Muslim Pakistanis, two Indians and eight 'Asians' qualified their ethnicity with 'British', none with English, Scottish, Welsh or Irish. The other Muslim self-descriptions are shown in the pie chart on page 134.

As well as the twenty who actually said they were white, it is possible that the twelve who called themselves English and indeed the 34 who said 'British' included some who were white. There is no way of telling. If they were not white, then this might be an indication of a fracturing of the racialised/ethnicised notion of what it is to be British/English already discussed. If they *are* white, this would further reinforce the point made earlier that English and British may

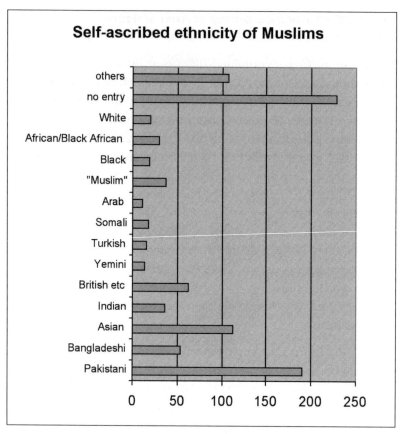

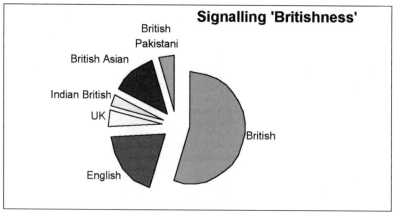

be excluding categories, being perceived as difficult to reconcile or merge with Islam.

Entries under *Hindu* contained significant numbers that were obviously meant to be humorous or offensive. About eight per cent were such spurious entries, far more than for either Sikhs or Muslims. Of the 247 entries taken seriously for analysis, a considerable majority thought of themselves as Indian or Asian, including the twelve who cited specific regions like the Gujarat, see below.

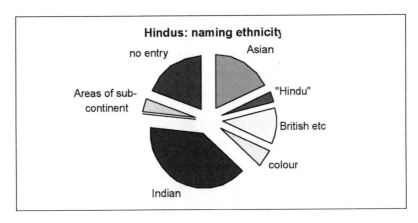

Under 'colour', five described their ethnic group as 'brown', four as 'black' and five as 'white'. They showed no other signs in their entries that suggested mischievous entries though I discounted many who did. The further five who described themselves as 'English' had nicknames resembling Hindu rather than Anglo-Saxon names, so it's reasonable to assume they are of immigrant descent. The 'British etc' category (n=29) had the following variations:

British	14	Anglo Indian	1
British Indian	2	Black English	2
British Asian	1	Half Welsh	1
English Indian	1	English	5
English Asian	1		

I speculated earlier about Sikhs having more of a symbolic connection to the geographic heartland of their faith than other south Asian groups, but in fact this turned out not to be so. Around 60 per cent of respondents from all three of the major south Asian faiths in Britain self-ascribed their ethnicity in terms of family roots rather than some variant on Britishness. This is markedly different from Modood *et al*'s finding, though the question was not put in the same way.

Self-ascribed ethnicity: Jews

Having considered the religious/ethnic self-ascription of south Asian people, it is logical to ask some of the same questions of Jews, especially as they, like Sikhs, are classified under British law as *both* religious and ethnic or racial groups. The population size here was 170.

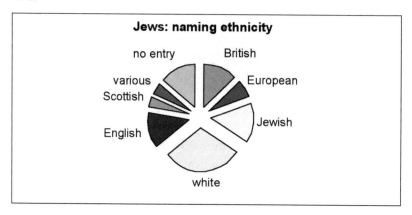

Not surprisingly given their length of residence in Britain, very few indicated national affiliations outside the UK. Though admittedly a small sample, a larger proportion of Jews than any other group identified their religion as also their ethnic group (15%). Two specific ascriptions merging different sorts of categories were 'Italian American Jewish' and 'European Anglo Jewish'.

Self-ascribed ethnicity: people of mixed descent

This emerged as new and growing category in the Census data in 2001, so it was considered important to consider separately the ways of describing 'mixedness'. Some hyphenated their descriptions, some used the word mixed, some said 'half....' At times it was difficult to distinguish someone who was saying they had one English parent and one Indian parent from a person of entirely Indian descent who described themselves as English Indian, so we cannot be sure that all these are correctly placed. Some people listed four roots, such as Colombian/Italian/Spanish/English or Italian/Jamaican/English/Polish, some three:

English Indian Iranian	1	English Italian Scottish	1
British Swedish Spanish	1	Canadian Irish English	1
English Californian Latin	1	German English Scottish	1
English French Irish	1	Russian Austrian Welsh	1
English German Italian	1	English Mexican American	1
English Italian Irish	1	Irish English Pakistani	1
English Jewish German	1	German English Indian	3

But most in this group straightforwardly named two national roots (where unstated it is assumed the unstated 'halves' are British):

English French	4		
Half French	1	Irish Indian	1
Half French half English	1	Half English half Indian	2
English German	4	Bangladeshi English	1
Half German	1	Welsh Hawaiian	1
English Italian	4	Iranian Scottish	1
Half Italian half English	2	Half Persian	1
English Polish	5	Half Iranian half English	1
Swiss English	2	Half English half Persian	1
Spanish English	3	Libyan Scottish	1
American English	14	Turkish English	2
English Australian	1	Mauritian Irish	1
Half Australian	1	Canadian Scottish	1
Malaysian Portuguese	1	Italian Scottish	1
Indian Pakistani	1	French Scottish	2
Spanish Filipino	1	Irish German	1
Jamaican Indian	1	Irish Greek Cypriot	1
Half Greek half British	1	Dutch Polish	1
Half Scottish half Spanish	1	French Polish	2
Half Scottish half English	1	Italian Spanish	1
Half Welsh half English	2	Half Mexican half German	1

The range of identities respondents were aware of and prepared to name suggests that for them at least these social and cultural rather than biological categories have some salience.

In addition to a couple who added 'white' to identities such as Scottish Canadian there were also many who employed colour or racial terms to describe their own mixed ethnicity. One small group of these were mixed 'Chinese', a term that, in practice, seems to be used racially rather like 'white', 'black' and sometimes 'European', in that most British Chinese people are not and have never been of Chinese *nationality*.

Chinese Irish	1	Asian Black Chinese	1
Chinese Indian	2	Black Chinese	1
Chinese White	2	Half Chinese	2
Chinese English	2		

Another group did not strictly speaking use 'colour' descriptions, but in the British context clearly signify it:

Caribbean Mix	1	European Indian	1
Afro Caribbean English	1	British European Asian	1
Irish Caribbean Welsh	1	Asian English	2
Irish West Indian	1	Asian European	2
English West Indian Asian	1	Pakistani Arab	1
IndoAnglo Caribbean	1	Half African	2
Caribbean Indian	2	British half Indian Scottish	1

Finally, there is a group who used 'colour' words explicitly. Several of these categories could have been combined, but they have been left as originally written to reflect what was presumably important to the respondents: whether they describe their parentage as black/white or white/black is probably not arbitrary.

Black White American	1	Eurasian	9
Black White British	1	White Black African	1
Black White	7	Coloured English	1
White Black	1	Black Asian	2
Half Black	2	Half White Half Brazilian	1
Asian White	1	Half White Half Indian	1
Black White Asian	1	Half Malaysian Half White	1
Indian White	1	Half Oriental Half White	1
White English Asian	2	Black Korean	1
White Brown	3		

Despite being disliked for some years, largely informed by black and minority ethnic commentators, the description 'half-caste' was used surprisingly often:

Half Caste	27
Halfcaste British	2
Halfcaste Middle East English	1

Only one person used the term 'dual heritage', yet it is seen as the preferred term by many commentators and professionals.

Self-ascribed ethnicity in terms of religion

I was aware that even with a free choice of how to self-describe on the log-in screen ethnicity was still prioritised as an aspect of identity that some users might not feel. One reason explored by Modood (1992) is the salience of the category to individuals and groups, so 'Muslim' may be a much more significant way of self-identification a – 'mode of being' – rather than race or colour, which is defining oneself in terms of the mode of oppression. Despite this forcing of users into pre-set categories, relatively few named their religion as their ethnicity, but the minority ethnic respondents were *relatively* more likely to do this than those who identified themselves 'ethnically' as Christians of various kinds.

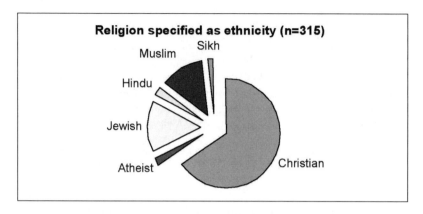

Why Christians in Britain would perceive their religion as their ethnicity is puzzling, although the two are often explicitly combined by the extreme Right. A few gave their location as Northern Ireland, where in effect Catholicism or Protestantism *is* ethnicity.

Self-ascribed ethnicity: intriguing entries

Some of the entries were intriguing. The meanings and realities behind them could only be guessed at. Remembering the question 'How would you describe your ethnic group?' I wondered what lay behind these entries and to which ethnic groups they belonged:

Not very good	1
Powerful	1
OK	7
The best	7
Great	8
Good	11
Not bad	72
Basic	1
Strange	4

Conclusions

So what can we tell from this? One obvious conclusion is that the results are indicative of the huge complexity of ethnic naming and underlines the range of self-ascriptions people draw from. These involve national origins, parental roots, geographical regions, religion, colour and, evidently, knowledge of how one is perceived by others.

Little has been said here about the purposes of official classification and counting, except in some oblique references to discrimination. This is not the place to argue it, but I believe that without such classification and counting, no reliable data is possible about discrimination against minority ethnic people, so the attempt is certainly worthwhile. This is a view well consolidated in British and US policy debate, but much less so within mainland Europe. However, the Office of National Statistics and public bodies who have a need to classify populations to promote social justice have an increasingly complex task on their hands, given the multitude of ways in which people describe themselves.

Section IV
Sketching pictures for improvement

10

Young people's experience of compulsory schooling in England and Scotland over twenty years of educational reform

Linda Croxford

Senior research fellow at the Centre for Educational Sociology of the University of Edinburgh, Scotland

Introduction

This chapter reviews the changes in young people's experiences of schooling in the last two decades in Britain. It examines changes in the outcomes of schooling – rising levels of attainment and increasingly positive attitudes to school – in a context of immense policy change in education. In Britain, as in many systems throughout Europe and beyond, neo-liberal design principles of marketisation, competition, standardisation, differentiation and so on were implemented during this period (Minguez and Murillo, 1996), and are associated with deepening inequalities and tendencies to polarisation (Lindblad and Popkewitz 1999). The current study explores these wider social justice concerns through its comparative dimension.

The two countries in question in this chapter – England and Scotland – offer scope for internal comparison as, although they are part of the UK, they have separate education systems whose distinctive character has long been recognised. The creation of a Scottish Parliament has the potential to translate into action different policies on issues of social justice. Wales was included in the overall comparative study, as was an analysis of gender differences, but this chapter focuses solely on social class differences between England and Scotland.

The key differentiating factor for this analysis is the extent of comprehensive school provision – that is to say, secondary schools which do not select pupils by ability. Critics of marketisation suggest that its emphasis on competition and differentiation advantages middle class parents and pupils who know how to work the system, while working class or less advantaged families lose out. Advocates of comprehensive provision maintain that it is better and fairer (McPherson and Willms, 1987). Scottish provision is almost entirely comprehensive, while England has become more and more diversified in the period under review, with an increase in complex forms of selection.

So the key social justice related questions here are: Did comprehensive provision in Scotland reduce social class related disadvantage? Did this social class gap close more than in England or less?

The empirical evidence to address these questions comes from time-series data derived from the England and Wales Youth Cohort Study and the Scottish School Leavers Surveys.

Social change

During the 1980s and 1990s the cumulative effects of social change originating earlier in the century had their impact on school systems. For example, changes in the industrial structure of Britain have been characterised by decline in manufacturing industry and a concomitant decline in the proportion of workers in manual occupations. More of the work force are engaged in white-collar jobs, and the growing number of managers and professionals within their ranks reflect the increasingly complex division of labour based on scientific and capital-intensive technology (Halsey, 2000). The importance of the education system in developing the skills and talents required in the knowledge-based economy was first emphasised in

1976 by Prime Minister James Callaghan when he initiated the 'Great Debate', and has been re-iterated by policy makers many times. Similarly, young people and their parents have increasingly been made aware of the importance of educational qualifications as a means of accessing career opportunities.

Education policies in previous decades have also had cumulative effects on social change. In particular, the increased provision of free public education after the war, and subsequent raising of the school leaving age to 15 in 1947, and 16 in 1972, has ensured that the parents of school pupils have themselves experienced higher levels of education. The reorganisation of schools on comprehensive lines from 1965-80, although contested and incomplete in England, was an important step in reducing social class barriers in education. These policies are linked to social mobility, as Halsey observes:

> By the end of the century millions of children of manual workers had risen into non-manual jobs and many thousands had become the graduate grandchildren of butchers, bakers and candlestick makers, following professional careers. (Halsey, 2000:17)

However, there are still major class inequalities in British society, and this chapter considers the changes during the last year of compulsory schooling.

Differences between England and Scotland

The education systems of England and Scotland share many common features which appear to reflect distinctively British patterns of attainment, participation and transition (Raffe *et al*, 1999). There are, however, small but significant differences. Figure 1 summarises the structure of British education systems. In each system compulsory schooling starts at about age 5, and ends at about age 16. There is a transition from primary to secondary school at age 11 in England and at age 12 in Scotland. Secondary schools in all the British systems provide general education, and there is no division between academic and vocational institutions as elsewhere in Europe. At age 16 young people can choose to continue their education at school or college, or to enter youth training or employment. At the beginning of the 1980s there was a strong tradition of entry to

Figure 1: The structure of British education systems

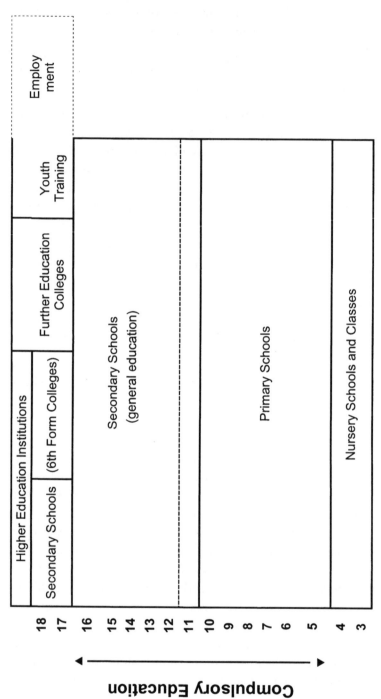

the labour market at 16, but this has diminished over the two decades, as a result of social and economic change.

A key difference between the school systems of England and Scotland arises because in Scotland secondary schools are more comprehensive, and characterised by more social mixing and greater equality of attainment, compared with the diverse range of state schools in England. After 1965, comprehensive reorganisation proceeded far more rapidly in Scotland than in England, so that by 1980 almost all pupils in state-funded schools in Scotland were attending schools that were at least nominally comprehensive, compared with 83 per cent in England. There are still areas of England that retain selective systems of secondary schooling. The fee-paying sector is larger in England than elsewhere in Britain – eleven per cent of pupils in England attend fee-paying schools compared with six per cent in Scotland. In England there are also more single-sex and faith schools. An earlier study, based on data for 1990/91, found that schools in Scotland were similar in their effectiveness whereas schools in England had greater variability, and concluded that because the school effect is more uniform, comprehensive education may be more effective and receive more public support in Scotland: finding the right school is less important (Croxford, 2000a).

Reforms in the 1980s and 1990s

During the 1980s and 1990s administrative reforms were put into place which further affected young people's experience during the final stages of compulsory schooling, namely

- the introduction of common core curriculum
- common systems of assessment and certification at age 16
- creation of quasi-markets in education.

Introduction of common core curriculum

The introduction of national curricula in the 1980s demonstrates the more consensual approach to policy making in Scotland compared with the more overtly political approach in England. In Scotland, a common curriculum framework was introduced on an advisory basis in 1983, recommending that students choose subjects within a number of modes. By contrast, the National Curri-

149

culum for England was made statutory in the 1988 Education Reform Act, and specified the number of subjects that must be studied (Croxford, 2000b). Linked to the National Curriculum in England was a mandatory system of National Testing at key stages, with results published on a school-by-school basis as part of a quality assurance system. In Scotland, by contrast, the introduction of National Testing was strongly resisted by parents' groups as well as teachers, and a much more flexible system was introduced that could be used at the teachers' discretion.

Common systems of assessment and certification at 16

National examinations at 16 serve similar purposes throughout Britain of providing a common system of certification of achievement at the end of compulsory schooling. These examination certificates are important credentials for young people entering further education or the labour market. But the systems of examination in place at the beginning of the 1980s had been designed to cater for the top third of the ability range and were inappropriate for all students. The division of students between certificate and non-certificate classes was very selective and demotivated pupils. The introduction in 1986 of the General Certificate of Secondary Education (GCSE) in England and Scottish Certificate of Education (SCE) Standard Grade in Scotland provided systems of certification for a far wider range of abilities, and thus greater motivation for students. Initially, both GCSE and Standard Grade included assessment of course work as a component of the final grade, and this is still the case in the Scottish examinations. However, in England there has been increasing emphasis on external examinations, and erosion of the role of course work, because of anxieties about standards.

Creation of quasi-markets in education

The restructuring of education through market principles and competition between schools has been more far-reaching in England than in Scotland (Ozga and Lawn, 1999). A result of the operation of market principles in England is that social segregation between schools increased (Croxford and Paterson, forthcoming). Following the creation of the Scottish Parliament in 1999 the systems are exhibiting signs of increased divergence. For example, Scotland has discontinued the publication of school league tables, and Scotland does not favour the policy of creating specialist schools, whereas their publication continues in England, which is likely to erode the provision of comprehensive schooling in England still further.

The time-series datasets

The data used for the analyses are derived from two cohort survey series which have common origins: the Scottish School Leavers Surveys and the England and Wales Youth Cohort Study (Croxford, 2006). These postal questionnaire surveys cover nationally-representative samples of young people in the last year-stage of compulsory schooling – Year 11 in England and Secondary 4 in Scotland. Some questions in the two are similar, and they permit comparative analysis, including attitudes to school, attainment in national examinations at the end of compulsory schooling and social class.

However, limitations on the social class data for England mean that the results have to be treated with caution (Croxford, 2006). Whereas for the Scottish time series the detailed questions about parental occupation have been consistently coded to the full occupational classifications developed by the Office for National Statistics (ONS), the coding of parental occupation in the YCS has been inconsistent and incomplete. We have tried as far as possible to use the occupation data to create social class variables that are consistent over time and between the two survey series, but we must be cautious in interpreting the findings on national differences in social class inequalities prior to 1990.

Changes and inequalities in attainment at age 16

A key outcome of schooling for young people in Britain is attainment in national examinations at 16. Once GCSE and Standard Grade examination were introduced almost all students sat these examinations, so we can analyse changes and inequalities in attainment. Overall upward trends in attainment are illustrated in Figure 2.

The attainment score shown in Figure 2 is based on all GCSE or Standard Grade examinations attempted by young people in the survey, allocating 7 points for A or 1, 6 points for B or 2, 5 points for C or 3, 4 points for D or 4, 3 points for E or 5, 2 points for F or 6, and 1 point

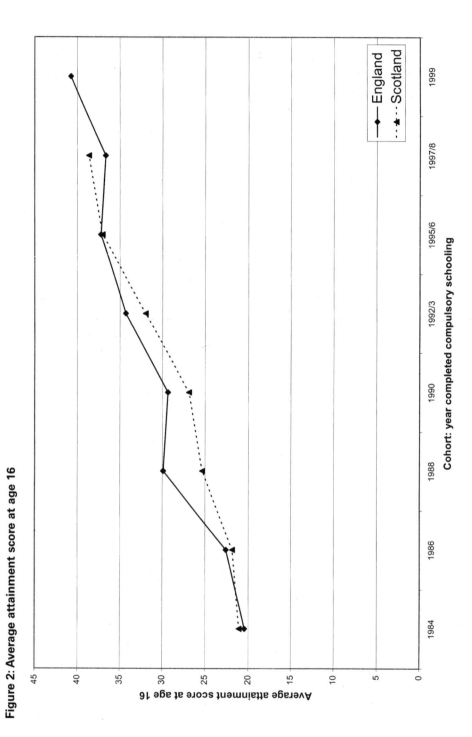

Figure 2: Average attainment score at age 16

for examinations attempted for which the result was lower than F. On average, students in Scotland attempted one fewer examination than their counterparts in England and consequently their average attainment scores were a few points lower.

A key issue for the analysis is the relative trends for students of different social class background. We know that social change has brought about changes in the family context of students, and we need to take this into account. The Scottish time series includes fairly detailed information about family background that is not available for the English time series. Therefore the first analysis of changes in attainment is based solely on the Scottish series, and then trends are compared with more limited information for England.

The effects of family background in Scotland
Analysis of family background data from the Scottish time series shows:

- a growing proportion of young people had parents who had been educated beyond the minimum school leaving age – just 16 per cent of the 1984 cohort had one or more parents who left school at age 17 or later, compared with 41 per cent of the 1998 cohort
- a growing proportion of young people had a parent in a professional or managerial occupation – 23 per cent in 1984 compared with 36 per cent in 1998
- a growing proportion of young people had both parents in full-time employment – among the 1984 cohort 74 per cent of fathers and 30 per cent of mothers were reported to be in full-time employment compared with 81 per cent and 45 per cent respectively among the 1998 cohort
- the proportion with mothers full-time unpaid in the home decreased from 25 per cent in 1984 to 11 per cent in 1998
- there was a slight decline in the proportion of young people staying with both natural parents – as opposed to step or lone parents from 79 per cent in 1984 to 74 per cent in 1998.

These changes in family background raise questions about the nature of inequalities over time. For example, if more young people have well educated parents, does parental education still provide a source of advantage for pupils? And, conversely, does greater disadvantage accrue to pupils with less educated parents?

A regression model tested the extent to which there were inequalities in young people's attainment scores associated with family background, and the extent to which their effects changed over time. The detailed results are shown in Appendix 1. These findings make clear that in Scotland there was a measurable reduction in the effects of social class background on attainment at the end of compulsory schooling.

The analysis shows that on average attainment was:

- lower if parents left school at the minimum school leaving age
- lower if parents' occupations were working class or unclassified occupations social class – and, to a smaller extent, intermediate
- lower if a parent was unemployed, or if the father was working part-time or full-time unpaid at home
- higher if the mother was working part-time or full-time unpaid at home
- lower if the young person lived with a step-parent or lone parent or neither parent.

Over the period from 1984 to 1998 the effects of these factors on attainment changed as follows:

- the effect of parents' school-leaving age diminished
- the disadvantage of working class and unclassified parental occupation diminished
- the disadvantage of an unemployed parent diminished
- the advantage of mother working part-time or full-time unpaid at home diminished
- the effects of step and lone parents and neither natural parent remained unchanged.

In other words, the changing social context in which more parents are better educated and more are in white-collar jobs appears to have reduced social class inequality in Scotland. The effects of social class in England and Scotland are now compared.

The effects of social class in Britain

In the YCS time series there is less information about family background than in Scotland. Consequently the comparison of trends and inequalities is limited to the social class of parental occupation. Detailed results are given in Appendix 2.

National system differences:

■ Attainment scores in Scotland were two points lower than in England – all other things being equal. The difference in Scotland arises from the smaller number of examinations attempted

■ Attainment increased substantially over the period 1984-1999, but the rate of increase was smaller in Scotland than in England.

Social class differences:

■ in both systems attainment was lowest among young people from working class backgrounds, and in England this effect did not change over time. But in Scotland the attainment gap associated with working class background did decrease over time

■ in 1984 young people with parents in intermediate occupations had lower attainment than those in professional and managerial occupations, but this gap decreased over time. In Scotland in 1984 the gap between intermediate and professional and managerial social classes was smaller than elsewhere, and although the gap decreased over time the rate of decrease was not as steep as in England

■ young people whose parental occupation was unclassified had lower attainment than those with parents in professional and managerial occupations. In 1984 this effect was greater in Scotland than in England, but over time the disadvantage accruing to unclassified social class in Scotland diminished.

In summary, trends and inequalities by social class are broadly similar in both national systems. However, in Scotland the inequalities associated with parents' social class lessened over the period.

How do young people perceive their school experiences?

Three questions about young people's perceptions of their last two years of compulsory schooling have consistently been included in the YCS for several years, and also in the Scottish surveys since 1992. These questions, which were typically the first items in the Sweep 1 questionnaire, asked:

> *Here are some things, both good and bad, which people have said about their last two years at secondary school. We would like to know what you think.*
>
> *Please tick a box for each one to say whether you agree or disagree.*
>
> ☐ School has helped give me confidence to make decisions
>
> ☐ School has done little to prepare me for life when I leave school
>
> ☐ School has taught me things which would be useful in a job.

Changes over time in responses to these questions are shown by Figures 3 to 5, and reveal that young people throughout Britain are becoming increasingly positive about their school experience. There is a clear upward trend in the proportions of young people who agreed that school taught them things which would be useful in a job, and a more modest increase in those who agreed that school helped give them confidence to make decisions. Similarly, increasing proportions of young people disagreed with the statement that school has done little to prepare them for life after school.

The overall trends towards more positive attitudes to school are evident in both education systems, but there are some system differences. There are no data on young people's attitudes in Scotland in the 1980s, but in the 1990s trends for Scotland are steeper than in

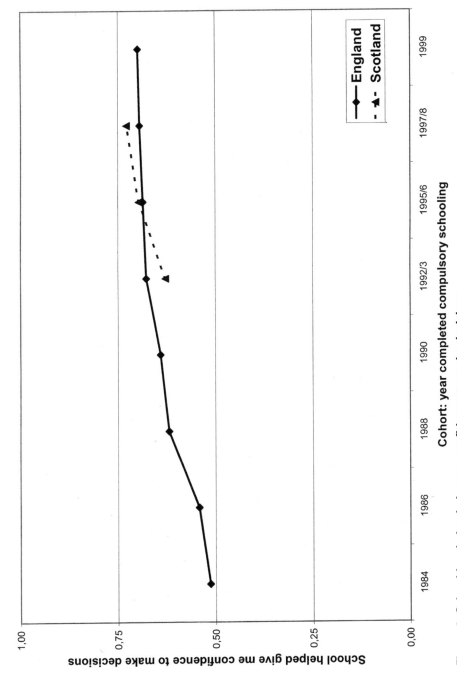

Figure 3: School has helped give me confidence to make decisions

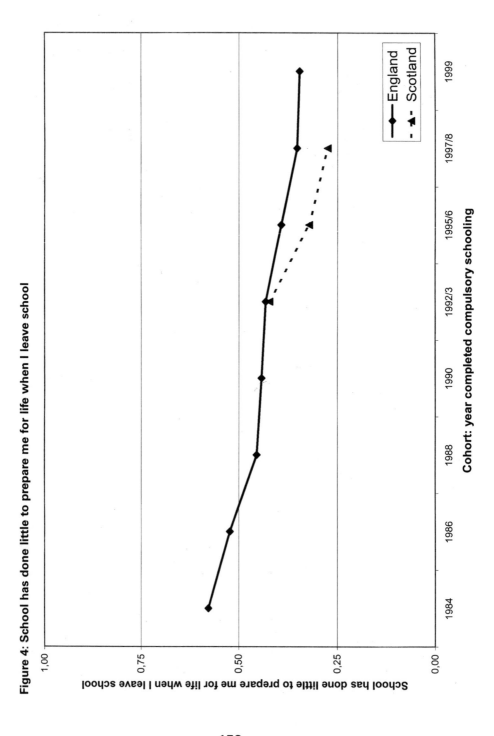

Figure 4: School has done little to prepare me for life when I leave school

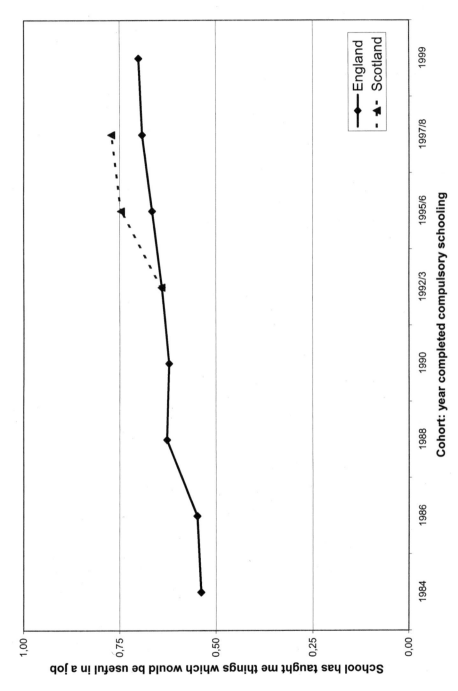

Figure 5: School has taught me things which would be useful in a job

England. In 1992 the proportion of Scottish youngsters expressing positive views of their schooling was similar to that in England, but thereafter increased much more steeply to 1998. Are these differences a commentary on the English and Scottish systems or are they consequences of compositional differences in socio-economic background?

A regression model was used to analyse differences in students' attitudes between the two systems (Appendix 3). The model confirms that on average attitudes to school improved steadily over the period, and that the upward trend was steeper in Scotland from 1992 onwards than in England.

Attitudes to school were strongly associated with parents' social class, with pupils from professional and managerial backgrounds holding the most favourable views. However, in Scotland the difference in attitudes between social class groups was significantly smaller than in England.

There was no evidence, however, that these average differences in attitudes between social class – and gender – groups changed over time. All groups, in all three systems, shared increasingly favourable attitudes to school.

Conclusions

This chapter has examined trends in young people's perceptions of their experience of school, and inequalities in their attainment during the 1980s and 1990s, in the light of social change and policy change.

The analyses show marked upward trends in attainment at the end of secondary schooling following the introduction of GCSE and Standard Grade examinations, and may demonstrate the success of educational reforms that have enabled more young people to achieve more highly.

The analyses show that young people are increasingly positive in their perceptions of the usefulness of school. This may demonstrate the impact of policies towards curriculum and assessment and the inclusion of all young people in national systems of certification. In contrast, in the late 1970s, before the introduction of GCSE and Standard Grade, young people in Scotland were asked their views of their school experiences. One young woman replied as follows:

> At our school we were put into groups one's who can sit their O grades and one's who can't which is unfair. The one's who did not sit there O grades the teachers never Bothered to learn them anything. The only good thing about the school was p.e. as that was the only class the teachers Bothered about us. The one's who were not in O grade classes never got to see anybody about a job for advice so no wonder pupils stade off as much. (Quoted in Gow and McPherson, 1980:29). (grammar and spelling uncorrected)

The increasingly positive attitudes of young people following the GCSE/Standard Grade reforms may result from a growing sense of achievement as more young people achieve success in examinations. However, social change may also have an impact, as there is growing awareness among young people that their future career prospects depend upon the academic skills and credentials that schools provide.

Young people from lower social class backgrounds tended on average to be less positive in their attitudes to school than those from higher social class backgrounds, and this may reflect a continuing sense of alienation from school. Interestingly, however, the increasing trends of satisfaction with school were found among all social class groups. There was no evidence of gender differences in attitudes to school, and the increasingly positive attitudes were shown by both boys and girls.

A key question for this research is whether the neo-liberal reforms of the 1980s and 1990s have eroded or increased existing social class inequalities in schooling at a time when the relative positions of social class groups are changing. There is strong evidence that the attainment gap associated with social class and other family background factors has diminished in Scotland. The trend of reducing inequality in attainment is less clear in England, and this may indicate that the different priorities of policy in Scotland have made a difference. Arguably the more comprehensive Scottish system and the more moderate marketisation have provided an environment in which working class pupils are enabled to catch up somewhat with their peers from higher social class backgrounds. But the stronger move to markets in England, and the resistance to such moves in Scotland, are themselves the product of broader cultural and political differences, and it is difficult to judge whether changing patterns of inequality are influenced by neo-liberal reforms or by those broader national differences.

Acknowledgement

This chapter is a product of the research project on Education and Youth Transitions in England, Scotland and Wales, 1984-2002, supported by the UK Economic and Social Research Council [R000239852].

Appendix 1

Scottish time-series: Change over time in effects of family background variables on attainment score at age 16

	Modelled separately		Modelled together	
	Estimate	Std. Error	Estimate	Std. Error
Family structure				
Reference category: Living with both natural parents, 1984 cohort	24.09	0.147	26.43	0.346
Step-parent	-5.42	0.597	-4.07	0.535
Lone parent	-6.76	0.394	-1.73	0.393
School hostel/boarding	7.47	1.157	1.79	1.040
Other	-10.67	0.789	-2.89	0.744
Average increase per year	1.34	0.018		
Additional effect per year of:				
Step-parent	0.06	0.067	0.05	0.060
Lone-parent	0.06	0.046	-0.07	0.046
School hostel/boarding	-1.71	0.161	-1.45	0.144
Other	0.06	0.099	-0.16	0.093
Age parents left school				
Reference category: Parents left school at 15, 1984 cohort	19.14	0.179		
One or both parents left school at 17+	16.52	0.338	10.51	0.347
One or both parents left school at 16	5.50	0.329	3.12	0.313
No information about parents' school leaving age	-1.37	0.409	-0.29	0.395
Average increase per year	1.27	0.030		
Additional effect per year of:				
parents left school at 17+	-0.49	0.042	-0.32	0.043
parents left school at 16	-0.30	0.042	-0.15	0.040
No information	0.16	0.051	0.12	0.049

	Modelled separately		Modelled together	
	Estimate	Std. Error	Estimate	Std. Error
Social class of parents' occupation				
Reference category: Professional and managerial, 1984 cohort	31.60	0.224		
Intermediate, small employers and own account workers	-4.88	0.333	-2.97	0.325
Working class	-14.92	0.300	-10.22	0.320
No information/ unclassified	-20.45	0.446	-13.42	0.493
Average increase per year	1.06	0.025		
Additional effect per year of:				
Intermediate,	-0.02	0.039	-0.03	0.038
Working class	0.31	0.037	0.20	0.040
No info/ unclassified	0.50	0.051	0.39	0.058
Parents' employment status				
Reference category: Both parents in full-time work	25.54	0.226		
Father part-time	-4.21	1.292	-2.36	1.178
Father full-time unpaid at home	-6.16	1.741	-3.85	1.590
Mother part-time	0.69	0.311	1.91	0.287
Mother full-time unpaid at home	0.66	0.330	1.87	0.305
One or both parents unemployed	-10.64	0.399	-5.28	0.380
Other (eg disabled, retired)	-7.06	0.360	-1.73	0.364
No information	-9.86	0.502	-3.69	0.503
Average increase per year	1.28	0.025		

Additional effect per year of:	Modelled separately		Modelled together	
	Estimate	Std. Error	Estimate	Std. Error
Father part-time	0.14	0.137	0.06	0.125
Father full-time unpaid at home	0.06	0.215	0.06	0.196
Mother part-time	-0.09	0.037	-0.11	0.034
Mother full-time unpaid at home	-0.13	0.046	-0.10	0.042
One or both parents unemployed	0.19	0.048	0.13	0.046
Other (eg disabled, retired)	0.34	0.047	0.15	0.046
No information	0.05	0.061	-0.02	0.078

Appendix 2

Britain: changes in attainment score associated with family background

	Estimate	Std.Error
National system		
Reference category: England	33.20	0.19
Scotland	**-2.22**	0.34
Change over time		
(Reference category: 1984 cohort)		
Average change per year	**1.17**	0.02
Scotland	**-0.19**	0.04
Parents' social class		
(Reference category: Professional and managerial)		
Intermediate, small employers and own account workers	**-8.23**	0.25
Working class	**-14.91**	0.25
Unclassified	**-2.88**	0.29
Additional effects of social class per year		
Intermediate etc	**0.08**	0.03
Working class	-0.04	0.03
Unclassified	0.00	0.03
Social class in Scotland		
Intermediate etc	**3.37**	0.44
Working class	-0.02	0.41
Unclassified	**-2.60**	0.56
Additional effects of social class in Scotland per year		
Intermediate etc	**-0.10**	0.05
Working class	**0.34**	0.05
Unclassified	**0.53**	0.06

Appendix 3

Factors influencing young people's attitudes to school
(estimates from linear regression model)

	Estimate	Std.Error
National System		
Reference category: England	1.62	0.01
Scotland	**-0.28**	0.05
Change over time		
(Reference category: 1984)		
Average change per year	**0.03**	0.00
Scotland	**0.03**	0.00
Parents' social class		
(Reference category: Professional and Managerial)		
Intermediate, small employers and own account workers	**-0.16**	0.02
Working class	**-0.15**	0.02
Unclassified	**-0.10**	0.02
Additional effects of social class per year		
Intermediate etc	**0.01**	0.00
Working class	0.00	0.00
Unclassified	0.00	0.00
Social class in Scotland		
Intermediate etc	**0.07**	0.03
Working class	**0.06**	0.03
Unclassified	**-0.07**	0.03

11

The education of Roma and Sinti children in Germany: choosing among alternative programmes

Amy Garrett Dikkers

Assistant Professor of Education at the College of
St. Scholastica in St. Paul, Minnesota, USA

The Roma, like other Gypsies and Travellers, have been discriminated against in all sectors of European society throughout history (Barany, 2000; Mirga and Cheorghe, 1997; Perkins, 1999; Yuen, 2000). Historically, they faced extreme prejudice in Central and Eastern Europe and migrated to Western Europe. But the move West has not saved the Roma from encountering discrimination and violence or bias against them in social sectors.

The Roma are a visible minority in Germany and receive much media and political attention. A European Union Minority Accession Programme (EUMAP) (2002) discussion of the treatment of Roma in Germany cites three public opinion polls, or surveys. These showed that in 1992, 64 per cent of Germans had an unfavourable opinion of Roma, higher than towards any other minority group; that in 1994, 68 per cent of Germans did not want Roma and Sinti as neighbours, and prejudice towards Roma still persisting in 2001. German Roma and Sinti were given official minority status in Germany in 1997. Although this official status signified a formal acceptance of Roma as a minority group, and Roma have been legally afforded all the protection such status provides, minority rights and rights for Roma are still almost untouched issues. As of 2002, there was minority rights legislation in only five of sixteen German states, and none of those legislative agreements explicitly mentioned Roma or Sinti (EUMAP, 2002).

Roma in Germany include long-time residents (often Sinti), refugees and asylum seekers, and recent immigrants from Central and Eastern Europe (CoE, 1995; Crowe, 2003). The German government estimates that the number of Roma and Sinti in Germany is upwards of 70,000. German Romany leaders, however, estimate 150,000 to 200,000, and this increases when all groups of legal, illegal, citizen, and non-citizen Roma are included. There are an estimated 100,000 non-resident Roma in Germany (EUMAP, 2002; Ringold, Orenstein and Wilkens, 2005). Because of the policy in Germany not to collect ethnic data, there is no empirical evidence to show continued discrimination towards Roma and Sinti in Germany. Anecdotal evidence and media coverage, however, suggests the Romany community in Germany continues to face disadvantages in employment, education, living conditions and other social areas (CoE, 2001; EUMAP, 2002; Liégeois, 1999; Perkins, 1999; Wal, 2004; Yuen, 2000).

Although no official data are available on the number or achievement of Roma minorities in formal education, the German government has acknowledged that inequalities in education exist for the Roma and must be addressed (EUMAP, 2002). The German government recently started supporting non-governmental organisation (NGO) initiatives for the education of Roma children, although this is not a widespread decision, as each state has made its own response. EUMAP (2002) suggests that what is needed is an evaluation of NGO initiatives directed towards Roma integration, an assessment of good practices for the education of Roma children and dissemination of those practices, and a comprehensive policy for providing financial resources to the successful initiatives.

Four programmes in Germany that serve the Roma and Sinti population were included in the current comparative study (see Garrett Dikkers, 2006 for the complete study results). Each had a specific focus: language, mediation, integration, and mobile schooling. This study provides a foundation for policy makers critically to analyse current practice as a basis for implementing new programmes for Roma education.

Each programme was analysed according to how it addressed issues of Roma education, specifically socialisation differences, language acquisition, non-attendance, and low parental involvement, based in part on issues of immigrant education in Germany discussed by Klopp (2002). The four programmes were also compared on Rogers' (1995) characteristics of innovation as they affect the potential adoption and diffusion of the programmes throughout Germany.

The programmes
Frankfurt – Schaworalle

Schaworalle includes (a) preschool and kindergarten; (b) a school programme that teaches alphabetisation, German, and basic skills for school access; (c) after-school care for older children attending regular German schools, with sport and activities; and (d) programmes to increase parental participation. Schaworalle primarily serves children who are refugees or asylum seekers, few of whom have the right to stay permanently in the country. At the time of the present study, there were over one hundred children associated with the school, most of them Roma of Romanian extraction.

Schaworalle's formal status is that of a *Kindertagestätte*, a combination of preschool and kindergarten. All of Schaworalle's students are registered in the cooperating German primary or secondary school and receive report cards from that school. The two official German teachers who work at Schaworalle technically work for those co-operating schools but are placed at Schaworalle.

Currently there is also a part-time special education teacher who works with primary school children who have special needs or whose skills are not up to grade level. In addition to the special education teacher, school leader, and two full-time teachers, Schaworalle's staff includes one full-time kindergarten teacher. There are also two part-time teacher assistants in the kindergarten, one deputy school leader (part-time), two Roma teacher assistants, one assistant teacher for the older pupils, and one computer teacher funded through a grant from a local NGO.

171

Kindergarten activities at Schaworalle are geared toward developing basic understanding of German and teaching social skills as well as handicrafts and music. Education in the primary and secondary school also offers the basics: German, reading, writing, mathematics and geography, plus English and computer skills courses for older students. The staff identify the primary goals of the education pro-gramme as to: take the children off the streets; provide students with skills with which they can 'negotiate through life'; teach the basics; prepare students to attend regular German schools; and provide opportunities for older students to have apprenticeships or take the school-leaving exam.

Berlin – Drei Linden Schule

The Drei Linden Schule is a Berlin primary school located across a highway from the Drei Linden Stellplatz, a campground for mobile Roma and Sinti families. The Drei Linden Schule serves Roma and Sinti who are residents of Germany and other European countries. Many of the children attend schools in the neighbourhood of their homes in other cities for the winter months.

The Stellplatz was initially just a place for Roma and Sinti Travellers to park their mobile homes, but over time it gained official status as a campground and the government installed water and power faci-lities on the grounds. Also on the grounds is a trailer where school sessions are held, and this features as another case in the present study. Some parents choose to have their children attend school on the Stellplatz, others want their children to attend regular German schools, in this case, the Drei Linden Schule.

Students at the Drei Linden Schule are enrolled in classes just like non-Sinti and Roma. When families arrive at the Stellplatz, they come to the school and register their children to attend class until they move to another location. When the school year begins, the teachers who have Roma or Sinti children enrolled in their classes receive a two-page sheet of information from the department of education about what to expect from these pupils, plus some details about their mobile lifestyle.

The Drei Linden Schule does not receive any additional funds or teacher hours for the education of Roma and Sinti children. On average, the principal expects six children to be in attendance from the months of April to October (with a break over the summer vacation). However, the children who attend in April are not necessarily the same ones who attend in September. School finances and teacher hours are planned during the summer months and, since it is never known exactly how many Roma and Sinti children will attend each year, the principal cannot request more money or hours.

Berlin – Stellplatz school

The Drei Linden Stellplatz school serves the same population of students as the Drei Linden Schule. Some Roma and Sinti parents do not want their children to attend German public schools. Caritas – an international charitable organisation with a branch in Berlin – and the Berlin Sinti and Roma Association advocated that a school be set up on the Stellplatz grounds to serve the educational needs of these children. A teacher from the local special education school comes daily to the Stellplatz and conducts lessons there.

The Stellplatz school has a set schedule of activities but the schedule shifts depending on the number of students who show up for instruction. On an average day during the course of this study (autumn 2005), the teacher at the Stellplatz taught basic literacy skills to preschool students from 9:00 to 10:30, reading with the children and offering opportunities for them to practise drawing and writing. She taught fifth grade students (11 and 12 year olds) from 11:00 to 1:00, when some older students also came for German instruction. One other student came at noon some days for general instruction and in the afternoon the teacher helped students who attended the Drei Linden Schule with their homework.

One Caritas social worker provides additional educational and extracurricular activities for the children in the afternoons. These activities are mostly arts and crafts and sport-based activities designed to teach the children basic skills through play. There have also been instances of families who wish their children to acquire a school-leaving certificate, which they cannot do from the school at the Stellplatz. These children attend classes at the local special education school and complete coursework and exams for their school-leaving certificate there.

Hamburg – School-based programmes

Roma and Sinti children in Hamburg are served primarily in school-based programmes in the normal German schools which provide cultural mediators in the form of Roma assistant teachers, teachers and social workers. The programmes are heavily language and culture based and are adaptive, changing to meet the needs of the children served by the schools. The majority of Roma and Sinti children in Hamburg served by this project are refugees and asylum seekers from Poland, Romania and former Yugoslavia. It is believed there are around 25,000 Roma and Sinti in Hamburg, of whom about 5,000 are children in the public schools.

Programmes for education for Roma and Sinti children in Hamburg fall under the administration of the Institute for Advanced Education in Hamburg, under the auspices of the Ministry for Education and Sport. Currently Hamburg has Roma and Sinti teacher assistants and mediators based in seven schools. In many cases a teacher assistant or mediator has a main school but also works in other schools in the district. For example, one mediator works in only one school but cooperates with many other social institutions, accompanying social workers and other employees on family visits and serving as an advocate for Roma and Sinti families.

The Roma and Sinti teacher assistants and mediators work in schools as social workers, translators, interpreters, classroom assistants, curriculum developers, *Ansprechpartner* (conversation partners) and *Vertrauenspartner* (trust partners). In some schools, Roma teacher assistants teach stand-alone classes in Romanes for the Roma and Sinti children. In other schools, teacher assistants help in classes with large numbers of Roma and Sinti children, translating, explaining foreign concepts and assisting with the learning of all the children. One Roma teacher assistant offers homework help for Roma and Sinti children and yet another offers music and dancing classes for all students, in which he teaches the children traditional Roma cultural arts.

Case analysis

Summary of findings for research question one – to what extent does each of these four programmes address issues of Roma education?

Language

Language problems across programmes vary according to the population served. German Sinti and Roma often have no problems with German since they have lived in Germany all their lives. Roma and Sinti who are asylum seekers, immigrants, and refugees come from throughout Central and Eastern Europe and speak various European languages and dialects of Romanes. Also, Romanes is traditionally an oral language so many pupils have the difficulty of learning to read and write in German. In all programmes, pupils are given help as needed with German as a second language. This study found that the programmes that most comprehensively addressed the language needs of the Roma and Sinti children included:

- teachers, assistants or social workers who spoke or understood Romanes
- a focus on German as a second language, providing specialised help for students whose German language skills were less advanced than those of their peers.

Schaworalle and Hamburg are the two programmes in the current study that offer both these language. They are unique in having employees who speak or understand Romanes and have offered Romanes classes, although only one teacher in Hamburg teaches Romanes lessons at the moment. Hamburg's teachers are also working together to create curriculum materials for use in the classroom in order to help the Roma and Sinti maintain their culture and traditions and in the hope of slowing the decay of Romanes.

Socialisation differences

All four programmes seek to address the need for basic academic skills. Often what pupils also lack is a sense of how to behave in school. Not knowing what is considered basic knowledge and acceptable behaviour often alienates the Roma children from the others.

Schaworalle, Hamburg and the Stellplatz offer the most individualised attention so that students can develop their basic skills. The three programmes differ, however, in their goal for addressing those needs. At Schaworalle, it is hoped that the pupils can gain enough basic and social skills to learn the cultural norms of school behaviour and manage at regular German schools. In Hamburg, students already attend regular German schools and teachers address basic needs in order to ease their integration. At the Stellplatz, the teacher tries to keep her pupils at the skill level of their peers to ease their re-entry into their winter schools, without focusing on socialisation differences. Schaworalle and Hamburg also specifically work with teaching basic social skills, teaching children about the behaviour expected in school.

Attendance

Poor attendance by Roma and Sinti children stems from two things: first, school is not a typical part of the Roma and Sinti culture and second, many parents associate school with authority and fear that their children will lose their culture and 'become German' if they attend school.

Schools with Roma teachers, mediators or social workers, as in Hamburg and Schaworalle, are the ones that address these issues most effectively in order to encourage Roma and Sinti families to send their children to school. Part of the responsibilities of the teachers or mediators in these two programmes is to contact parents in an effort to encourage regular attendance. Schaworalle and the Stellplatz have both created more flexible school schedules so as to accommodate Roma families who prefer less structured school settings. In all four programmes, teachers and staff cannot be certain about the attendance of their Roma and Sinti pupils. Some do not have a permanent right to stay in Germany; others attend school as tourists; others live mobile lifestyles. Such uncertainty demands flexibility from the teachers and increases the difficulties in curriculum and instruction planning.

Parental involvement

Traditionally, family is one of the most important aspects of the culture of Roma and Sinti. Parental involvement is important for encouraging attendance in school and supporting the children in the classroom. Teachers at Schaworalle and in Hamburg stress the importance of understanding the parental point of view. As an assistant teacher at Schaworalle explains: '[The kids] sometimes have a problem that the parents don't want them to go to school, to a normal school... and actually it's a first step for them to let them go to Schaworalle.'

Parental involvement in schools is welcomed by all programmes but is actively encouraged by only two of them. Although parents can be easily involved in the school activities on the Stellplatz, they seldom are, and the parents at the Drei Linden Schule are even more rarely involved in its activities. At Schaworalle, parents and members of the Roma community are involved in the school household. They work in the kitchen; they clean the building; they take part in school celebrations; and many parents, especially the mothers, spend the day at school with their children. Hamburg social workers often conduct home visits to meet the parents and answer questions about their children's school experiences.

Summary of findings for research question two – how do the programmes compare on characteristics of innovation pertaining to their diffusion throughout Germany?

Using Rogers' (1995) theory about the diffusion of innovations, the four programmes in the current study were analysed with regard to whether they possessed the characteristics that make it more likely for the innovations to be adopted and diffused. The basic idea behind Rogers' theory is that the rate of adoption of an innovation can be explained by five characteristics: relative advantage, compatibility, complexity, trialability, and observability. Innovations with a high degree of relative advantage, compatibility, trialability, and observability and a low degree of complexity are adopted more rapidly throughout society.

Relative advantage deals with benefits and costs of an innovation in terms of economic profitability and social prestige. Also, 'individuals

177

want to know the degree to which a new idea is better than an existing practice' (Rogers, 1995:216). Each programme in the current study can be seen as better than previous programmes. In most cases, these opportunities for education were often in special education schools or afforded no opportunities for education for mobile Roma and Sinti. No two programmes offer students the same opportunities, but three of the programmes reviewed provide one-to-one instruction to address specific learning needs. School employees in Hamburg and at Schaworalle also work with the community to increase understanding of the Roma culture and to help Roma families understand the culture of school.

Three of the programmes involve collaboration with local government, educational institutions or non-profit organisations. These partnerships offer relative advantage for policymakers as they allow for shared resources and responsibility. Two of the cases, Hamburg and the Drei Linden Schule, are situated in regular German schools, thus offering the same social prestige to Roma and Sinti pupils as that gained by the rest. Some children can obtain school-leaving certificates which provide a higher level of social prestige in German society as a whole.

Compatibility as a characteristic of innovation relates to the degree to which an innovation is consistent with existing socio-cultural values and beliefs, past experiences, and the needs of a population (Rogers, 1995). The Drei Linden Schule is the only programme that serves children from families who have a culture of attending school. Most families served by the other three programmes are fearful or uncertain about school. So a challenge for these programmes is explaining to parents what school involves and building their trust so they feel comfortable sending their children to school. Schaworalle, Hamburg, and, to a certain extent, the Stellpaltz take the cultural values of Roma and Sinti into consideration in their organisational structure and daily activities, and this makes them more compatible than the Drei Linden Schule, other German schools, or special education schools.

For policymakers, the Stellplatz school is the least compatible with current school practice. The other three programmes are partly or completely based on recognised educational structures. Each of the four programmes is somewhat incompatible with the methods of instruction and planning typically used by German teachers, and two demand great flexibility from the teachers.

Complexity is also important. The less complex an innovation the more likely it is to be adopted quickly and diffused throughout society. All programmes serve complex populations in terms of residency status in Germany, country of origin, and language spoken. Teachers in each programme also have complex roles requiring understanding of Roma culture and traditions and flexibility over attendance and curriculum planning. Decentralisation of the educational system in Germany means that practice and planning vary across districts. Policymakers must take account of organisational and instructional differences between districts when implementing programmes.

Trialability is linked to complexity, because it addresses whether or not the innovation can be experimented with on a limited basis (Rogers, 1995). Each programme began as a small trialable programme, evolving over years to the current structure. Policymakers considering implementing similar programmes can try out the programmes in pieces to see whether they work in different settings. Parents have the chance to try out all four programmes, but the flexible structure and environment of Schaworalle and the Stellplatz are more conducive to such experimentation.

Observability is connected with complexity and trialability as it is concerned with the perspective different stakeholder groups take of an innovation. An innovation which is visible to others, is observable, and can be communicated, is more likely to be adopted (Rogers, 1995). Parents in all programmes can observe the activities of the school in order to become more comfortable with sending their children. Schaworalle is the programme that has received the most attention from other educators, policymakers, and the media (Leidgeib and Horn, 1994 and Lindemann, 2005), although the Hamburg project (Lindemann, 2005) and the Stellplatz school have also been subjects of media reports. Results of the programmes are only anecdotal. None has been the subject of official evaluations to determine effectiveness or the effects on student achievement.

Conclusions

Of the four programmes, Schaworalle seems to meet the needs of the Roma and Sinti population most comprehensively by addressing issues of language, socialisation differences, attendance and parental involvement. Nonetheless, the Hamburg programme is more effective socially because children in the schools with Roma and Sinti cultural mediators are integrated with German students and students from other immigrant groups. This integration is beneficial for the growth of the children and their future hopes for employment and integrated life in Germany.

How effectively the four programmes address issues of Roma education influences the perceptions of their relative advantage and compatibility. Analysis of the programmes across Rogers' (1995) characteristics of innovation indicated that issues of relative advantage and compatibility were extremely important for the Roma and Sinti parents.

Issues of complexity, trialability, and observability do not greatly influence the families and are less important to them and to teachers than relative advantage and compatibility. Results show that programmes need to address the issues of Roma education if they are to be effective and accepted by the Roma community as options for the education of their children. Programmes need to be better than the earlier ones. They have to decrease discomfort on the part of Roma parents. The children must be made to feel more comfortable about school and it should provide social prestige for the Roma involved – these are aspects of relative advantages. And programmes for Roma education must be consistent with Roma cultural values, build on past experiences, and provide for the needs of Roma children – all these are aspects of compatibility. Schaworalle and Hamburg are the programmes most closely aligned with relative advantage and compatibility.

From the perspective of policymakers, however, complexity and trialability as well as issues of cost (relative advantage) and the socio-political context (complexity and compatibility) are significant determinants of adoption. Policymakers want programmes that are easy to implement, have significant return on investments, are supported in society and the political arena, and have observable results. What remains is the need for programmes that address the needs of the Roma population, thereby providing relative advantage and compatibility for Roma families that also can be diffused throughout German society.

Broader implications of the current study

This study supports research and theory around issues related to the improvement of immigrant education and correlates those findings with education for the Roma and Sinti. Specifically, this study supports Domínquez's (1999) findings that successful education of immigrants requires coordination with other social welfare institutions – broadened to include charitable organisations and advocacy groups – and also the need for teacher training on ethnic and cultural diversity.

Organisational suggestions for the education of Roma children (Beck, 1999; CoE, 1993; Liégeois, 1989, 1999; OSCE, 2003; Ringold, 2000; Smith, 1997) are also supported by the findings of this study. These suggestions are:

- providing preschool programmes – a strong relative advantage for families served by Schaworalle and the Stellplatz school

- providing mentoring, extracurricular activities and tutoring to help reduce the number of dropouts – relative advantages for families served by Schaworalle, the Hamburg programme, and the Stellplatz school

- working to reduce discrimination and placement of Roma and Sinti students in special schools – in which Hamburg and Schaworalle show success

- providing teacher support – as done through partnerships with Roma assistant teachers and social workers in Hamburg and at Schaworalle.

One striking finding is that most employees in individual programmes had no awareness of other models for Roma and Sinti education in Germany. The socio-political context, lingering racial prejudice, and, ironically, pressure from international organisations

181

to provide for the education of Roma and Sinti have led to individual cities creating programmes that seem to fit with their specific needs instead of basing their decisions on theory or models of effective practice. One way this can be addressed is by establishing a federal office for support and information on Roma and Sinti education, bringing Roma education to the forefront, connecting individual programmes, and helping the diffusion of models of effective education throughout Germany. Similarly, most of the stakeholders I interviewed were unaware of actions or programme models in Europe for the education of Roma and Sinti. An informational office at federal level could have a core research and resources library where information about other programmes could be gathered and disseminated.

The study fits with Rogers' (1995) characteristics of innovation that leads to diffusion and Klopp's (2002) issues of immigrant education: the programmes for Roma education in Germany which have strong relative advantage and compatibility and address the needs of the population are the most effective. This research into four separate programmes supports this. But the most effective programmes for Roma education are not necessarily those most easily adopted and diffused throughout German society.

What is needed is an alignment of the implementation needs of policymakers and government officials with the desires of the families and individuals in the programmes. This would strengthen the possibility to develop programmes that offer parents high relative advantage and compatibility without sacrificing characteristics considered necessary for adoption by German policymakers and local governments. Better schools for Roma students can also be better schools for all pupils, providing cultural mediators and incorporating more cultural discussion into the classroom can promote the valuing of all cultures represented in a society and support mutual understanding amongst groups in society as a whole, so providing relative advantage and compatibility for all children.

12

Tense situations in ethnically diverse classrooms

Yvonne Leeman
Senior Lecturer at the Department of Educational Sciences,
University of Amsterdam and Professor of Teacher Education at
Windesheim University, The Netherlands
Hester Radstake
is a doctoral student in education, at the University of
Amsterdam, The Netherlands

Introduction

Dutch schools are becoming increasingly diverse, especially in the major cities. The changing ethnic demographics of schools all over the country are the result of labour migration (mainly from Turkey and Morocco), immigration by citizens from former Dutch colonies (Surinam and the Dutch Antilles), and the arrival of political and economic refugees (mainly from Africa and the Middle East).

One response to the increased heterogeneity of the pupil population has been intercultural education. But this has changed intrinsically under the influence of the hardening political climate on immigration and the multicultural society. Whereas the emphasis was previously on interpersonal relationships between pupils and respect for diversity, in the last few years the aim of assimilating immigrant pupils has become more important (Leeman and Pels, 2006). Nowadays a problem-oriented approach dominates educational policy in the field of ethnic diversity. The emphasis is on the problems of immigrant youth regarding their behaviour and cultural perspectives. A corrective, restrictive policy to stimulate assimilation of the problematic ethnic minority youth has been launched (Ministerie van Onderwijs Cultuur en Wetenschappen, 2004). There is anxiety about the incompatability of norms and values and about radical Islam.

While immigrants' experiences of tensions at school, for example discrimination and exclusion, have generally not been taken seriously, much attention has recently been paid to conflicts in mixed schools. Incidental reports about conflicts based on the experiences of teachers and headteachers often prompt the suggestion that safety is at risk and that the tensions are closely connected with the composition of the school population and the problematic behaviour of the immigrant youth. However, stress and conflicts are normal in any school. Systematic large-scale studies on whether extra or other tensions do arise in ethnically diverse classrooms, including teachers' experiences of such tensions, do not exist in the Netherlands.

Research on teachers shows that the tensions they experience in the classroom generally threaten values like justice, concern for others and sincerity (Maslovaty, 2000; Oser, 1991; Tirri, 1999). In their reactions – or non-reactions – to tense situations, teachers pass on moral messages (Hansen, 2001). These indicate that what is important in the way people deal with each other or, in the broader sense what is important for good citizenship. Accordingly, how teachers react or do not react to ethnic-cultural tensions is meaningful in the framework of intercultural education.

As knowledge based on systematic research on tensions experienced by teachers in ethnically mixed classes was unavailable, we undertook a nationwide survey. We present the results here. This survey is the first part of a larger research project on tense situations in ethnically diverse classrooms. The second part of the research consists of an interview and observation study into teaching practices in these classes.

Tense situations and teachers' experiences

Noticing tense situations, assessing their significance, understanding their context, and choosing how to react to them are important teaching competences (Leeman, 2006). Henze *et al* (2000) showed that headteachers who were involved in the quality of ethnic relations between pupils at their schools had a more complex understanding of intercultural conflicts than the usual interpretation of 'overt hostility'. They were more aware, for example, of the underlying tensions and causes of open conflicts. To develop a commitment to intercultural issues and diversity, life experiences with ethnic diversity are important, for example, in the context of family, friendships, education or work (Paccione, 2000). Theoretically, intercultural sensitivity is regarded as a requisite basis for developing the competences for teaching in ethnically diverse classes (Villegas and Lucas, 2002; Cochran-Smith, 1995).

Leeman (2006) carried out an interview study on eleven secondary-school teachers and the intercultural dilemmas they experienced in their mixed classrooms. She interviewed experienced teachers who were interested in intercultural issues. These teachers mentioned tense situations in which values like justice, respect for the school and the teacher, democracy, personal autonomy, diversity and communality were threatened. They pointed out new value dilemmas, such as balancing communality and diversity, and gave a special ethnic-cultural dimension to values already known to be the possible cause of conflict in the classroom. Justice is, for example, an issue when teachers are confronted with what they see as unfair accusations of discrimination by pupils, for example, over marking their work. It is also at stake when pupils make discriminatory remarks about someone's appearance or cultural background. Respect for the school and the teacher is particularly at risk when pupils break school rules on cultural grounds or do not want to accept the authority of the teacher.

The teachers, placing a great deal of value on personal autonomy, experience tensions between a personal critical stance and group loyalty, for example, in lessons dealing with politically sensitive topics like the Middle East. The teachers are generally concerned about the balance between communality and diversity in their

185

classes. They want to solve problems in a democratic way with the active participation of all pupils. However, the teachers' experience is that not all pupils are prepared to search for a solution together.

The interview study gave insight into the range of tensions teachers may find when teaching in ethnically mixed classes. The teachers interviewed do see ethnic-cultural differences between pupils but emphasise similarities. They distance themselves from the negative image forming in society about immigrants. They are very careful about labelling a particular group of pupils as a problem group. Their solutions do not follow the current trend of stricter rules and transfer of desired norms and values, but focus on dialogue. Given their interest in intercultural issues and their sensitivity to inter-cultural tensions, the teachers interviewed might be special. In the survey study we wanted to identify which tensions the average teacher of ethnically diverse classrooms experiences and whether they relate these tensions to the composition of their class.

Deciding how to react to tensions is not easy. Husu (2002) pointed out that many of the value dilemmas experienced by teachers re-mained unsolved. The willingness of teachers to react to tense situa-tions and how they react says something about the professionalism of teachers and about how they perceive their role as a moral agent (Walker and Snarey, 2004). When they notice a tense situation teachers must first decide whether to react or not. If they decide to react, their next decision is how to react, for example by expressing their own point of view, by acting in a punitive way or by merely ex-plaining their opinion about an incident without entering into dis-cussion with pupils. From the perspective of intercultural education, a dialogue is preferable when reacting to intercultural tensions (Burbules and Bruce, 2001; Parker, 2003). A genuine dialogue in the context of diversity is characterised by deliberation, based on the principles of social justice, inclusion and actual exchange (Parker, 2003).

The aim of the survey study was to find out not only what tense situations teachers in ethnically mixed classes say they have ex-perienced and whether they relate these to the ethnic mix, but also how they react to these situations. Moreover, we wanted to analyse whether personal characteristics such as age, sex, ethnic back-ground, experience of teaching in ethnically heterogeneous classes, and intercultural sensitivity are related to the tensions teachers experience. Context characteristics, such as type of education, ethnic composition of the class and level of urbanisation, may also affect teachers' experiences of tense situations. Leeman's study showed, for example, that tensions that undermine respect for the teacher and the school were mainly experienced by teachers in pre-voca-tional secondary education. According to the teachers, this was partly due to the lack of prospects for pupils in the lower vocational streams, the demotivating practice of transfer to a lower level of education and the lack of facilities for schools and teachers to build up a personal relationship with pupils. Pre-vocational secondary education has to cope with the stigma of being a 'reservoir for problems' (Kleijer *et al*, 2004). This is often related to the relatively high percentage of immigrant pupils in this type of education. Lastly, the kind of tensions that teachers experience can differ according to the environment where the school is located. For example, the problems in the Netherlands with pupils who wore Lonsdale clothes as an expression of their hostility to ethnic minorities mainly occurred in smaller cities and towns (Homan, 2006). A possible explanation for this is that pupils in those towns are not used to living in an ethnically mixed environment.

Research design

In search of the average teacher of ethnically mixed classes, our aim was to select half the schools from the four big Dutch cities and the other half from middle-sized cities and towns. We tried to involve 35 schools and three teachers per school and wanted the research group to reflect the national composition of the pupil population. Hence 60 per cent would be classes providing pre-vocational secon-dary education and 40 per cent providing general secondary educa-tion. We selected a stratified sample so that the proportion of immigrant pupils was evenly distributed between the various types of education. This made it possible to analyse the influence of the types of education and ethnic class-composition separately. On the whole we realised these selection criteria. In the end, 87 teachers returned the questionnaire (response 76%). The number of teachers varies in the results presented here, as not everyone answered all the questions.

Characteristics of the teachers

Fifty five per cent of the teachers were male. Thirty one percent were younger than 35 years old; 22 per cent were between 35 and 40 years and 47 per cent were over 45 years of age. Eighty percent of the teachers were of Dutch descent, based on the country of birth of both parents. The parents of the other teachers were born outside the Netherlands: six per cent of them in Western countries and fourteen per cent in non-Western countries, like Morocco and Surinam. Seventy one per cent of the teachers had more than five years' teaching experience and only seven per cent had two years or less. A large majority (66%) reported that they had considerable experience with teaching ethnically diverse classes, whereas 23 per cent reported that they had little experience, and ten per cent of the teachers said they had no earlier experience (n=87).

Characteristics of the classes

The ethnic background of the pupils in the research group was representative of the different ethnic groups living in the Netherlands. The percentage of immigrant pupils was divided equally over the different educational tracks, taking into account the 61-39 per cent division of the types of education.

Regarding the level of urbanisation, 41 per cent of the teachers taught classes in the four big cities and 59 per cent in smaller cities and towns. The percentage of immigrant pupils was higher in the classes in the four large cities (Cramer's V= 0.75; p<0.01), which reflects the picture nationwide.

Operationalisation of tense situations

From Leeman's interview study we selected 20 situations that teachers experienced in the classroom and that represent the whole range of value dilemmas they mentioned. The situations concern either the contact between the teacher and pupils or between the pupils themselves. They included general contact situations and situations that arise during class discussions. The situations reflect different positions on the dimension of underlying or open tensions and differed in intensity (Henze *et al*, 2000). An open situation is for example 'pupils refused to co-operate with certain pupil(s) when they should have'. There are underlying tensions in a situation such as when: 'one or more pupils did not dare to participate in a class discussion, because they had a different opinion on the subject than the majority'.

We formulated the situations in such a way that they may be typically experienced in any class. Some situations feature cultural or religious issues. However, what the value conflict is actually about is not specifically stated in these cases, for example, the situation: 'pupil(s) did not respect other pupils when discussing political or religious subjects'. We asked teachers how often they had experienced the situations (1= never; 2= sometimes; 3= often) and how stressful they found the situations (1= not; 2= slightly; 3= extremely). We also asked if they thought a situation was connected with the ethnically heterogeneous pupil population of the class (1= not, 2= slightly, 3= extremely) and how difficult they found it to decide how to react to the situation (1= not, 2= slightly, 3= extremely). The teachers were also asked to describe a situation they themselves had experienced but that was not included in the questionnaire.

We based the operationalisation of teachers' actions in tense situations on the earlier research of Oser and Althof (1993), Veugelers and De Kat (1998), Klaassen and Leeferink (1998) and Maslovaty (2000). For each situation teachers had experienced we asked them whether they had reacted to the situation, when and their reasons for their reactions. The answers possible were: I did not say or do anything, because I did not think it was necessary; I did not say or do anything, because I did not know how to react; I came back to it later, because I did not immediately know how to react; I came back to it later, because I thought that would be better; I reacted to the situation immediately and took no further action; I reacted to the situation immediately and came back to it again later.

We asked teachers to describe how they had reacted when this was the case. They could choose from several options: I had a talk with the pupils involved, in which I put across my own point of view; I had a talk with the pupils involved, without putting across my own point of view; I had a class discussion, in which I put across my own point of view; I had a class discussion, without putting across my own point of view; I punished the pupil(s) or sent them out of the class; I merely gave my point of view on the situation.

Fifteen teachers completed a draft questionnaire to ascertain whether they could sufficiently recognise the tense situations. We asked teachers to base their answers on their experiences in the current school year (2003/2004). They reported over a period of five to six months. Virtually nobody reported having experienced one particular situation so we excluded this from the analyses.

Intercultural sensitivity
Intercultural sensitivity has many aspects and we could not include all of these in the questionnaire. We used the scale developed by Chen and Starosta (2000) which focuses on the extent to which an ethnically heterogeneous context is valued. This scale consists of 24 items that are indicative of respect for cultural differences, inter-action confidence, interaction engagement, interaction enjoyment and interaction attentiveness. The original scale was developed for college students studying communication. We translated the original items into Dutch and reformulated them slightly, so they fitted the school context in the Netherlands and would be under-standable to teachers. Based on factor analysis on our data, 22 of the 24 items scored sufficiently highly (>0.3) on the first factor (un-rotated solution). These 22 items were therefore combined into one scale (Cronbach's alpha: 0.90).

Analyses
To find out which situations teachers experience, we checked the percentage of teachers who said they had at some time experienced a difficult situation. Given that the incidence – in the teachers' per-ception – of each situation was measured with a three-point scale on an ordinal level, non-parametrical tests were the most suitable for analysing differences between teachers. We analysed the relation-ship between personal and context characteristics on the one hand, and situations teachers experience on the other, with a Mann-

Whitney test when comparing two groups, concerning ethnic background, type of education, level of urbanisation. When comparing several groups on their teaching experience and experience of teaching ethnically heterogeneous classes, we used a Kruskal-Wallis test. We used the Spearman rank correlation to analyse the relationship between situations teachers experience on the one hand, and intercultural sensitivity and the percentage of immigrant pupils in the class on the other. With regard to the total number of situations teachers experienced, we used the t-test to compare two groups and the ANOVA to compare more groups. We analysed the relationship between teachers' intercultural sensitivity and the percentage of immigrant pupils in the class with the Pearson product moment correlation. With the help of teachers' mean scores, we analysed per situation how tense they found the situations, to what extent they related them to the ethnically heterogeneous class and how difficult they found them to deal with. We also calculated the percentage of teachers who chose each reaction specified in the questionnaire to the situation in question.

Results

Which tense situations do teachers experience in ethnically heterogeneous classes?

The percentage of teachers that indicate they have experienced a situation at some time varies from situation to situation, ranging from 13 per cent to 73 per cent (n=87). Open situations, such as when pupils broke school rules (73%; n=85) or refused to tell the truth to the teacher (for example, when something had been stolen at school and they did not want to betray the culprit) (71%; n=85), were mentioned most frequently. In most of the situations experienced, respect for the school or the teacher, or the balance between communality and diversity were threatened. Open and intense conflicts, for example when pupils intimidated the teacher or pupils drew a swastika, were reported by the lowest percentage of teachers (13%, n=82 respectively 13%, n=84).

Less than half of the teachers experienced situations referring to religious or cultural issues, mainly during class discussions. Examples of such situations include: 'pupils who excluded other pupils from a conversation in the classroom, because they felt that they had nothing to say about the subject, for example, because they did not belong to the group or were not religious' (13%; n=82) and 'pupils did not respect other pupils when discussing political or religious subjects' (24%, n=83).

Twenty eight teachers made use of the opportunity to describe a situation themselves that they had experienced. They did not mention new tensions.

Relationship between tense situations and personal and context characteristics

In none of the situations did we find differences between teachers on the basis of experience in teaching or experience in teaching ethnically heterogeneous classes. Immigrant teachers only differed from Dutch teachers in two situations concerning justice, namely 'pupils made a discriminatory remark about someone's appearance or cultural background during a class discussion' (z= -2.154; p<.05) and 'pupils made a contemptuous remark about someone's personal property because it was old-fashioned' (z=-2.932; p<.05). Fewer immigrant teachers had experienced these situations.

Teachers with a high level of intercultural sensitivity experienced fewer situations in total (r= -.33; p<.05). They experienced five situations less frequently (Spearman correlation varies from -.214 to -.283; p<.05). These reflected the whole range of situations that were presented.

Regarding the relation between teachers' experiences of tense situations and context characteristics, we found that more pre-vocational-education teachers experienced two situations about respect for the school and the teacher (z= -2.214 and z= -.198; p<.05).

Which situations cause teachers stress?

The degree of stress experienced by teachers differed from situation to situation, ranging from 1.31 to 2.09 (n varies from 11 to 61). The situations experienced by the fewest teachers were generally found to be the most stressful. As mentioned above, these were mainly intense open tensions in the contact between teachers and pupils and tensions between pupils over religious ideas or cultural issues, mainly during a class discussion.

Which situations do teachers relate to the ethnically mixed class?

The mean score for the question on whether teachers thought a situation was connected with the ethnically heterogeneous pupil population of the class ranged from 1.17 to 2.4 (n varies from 10 to 60). The situations many teachers experienced were the ones they related least to the ethnically heterogeneous composition of the class. Situations that arise during a class discussion and refer to cultural or religious issues were most strongly related to the ethnically heterogeneous class. Thirteen per cent to 46 per cent of the teachers experienced these situations (n=87).

Which situations do teachers find difficult to decide how to deal with?

The mean score to this question ranged from 1.14 to 2.00 (n varies from 10 to 56). The most difficulties were experienced in the intense situations that were infrequently experienced, such as when pupils intimidate teachers or accuse them of discrimination, followed by tensions during class discussions.

How do teachers react when confronted with tense situations?

Nearly all the teachers decided to react to a situation. More than 10 per cent of them said that they had not reacted because it was unnecessary in only four of the situations (ranging from 11 to 21%; n varies from 15 to 52). Tensions in these situations lay in the contact between pupils. In most situations the teachers reacted immediately. Sometimes they also came back to the matter later. Teachers decided to do so mainly when respect for the school or the teacher was at stake, or when cultural or religious issues play a role in the contact between pupils, for example, when 'pupils made a discriminatory remark about someone's appearance or cultural background during a class discussion'.

Most teachers reacted to the situations by having a talk with the pupils concerned in combination with a discussion with the class

(61% to 95%; n varies from 9 to 56), during which most of them expressed their own opinion. Few teachers punished the pupils (0% to 22%; n varies from 9 to 56), for example by sending them out of the classroom, or felt that giving their own opinion was sufficient (0% to 25%; n varies from 9 to 56).

Discussion

The media and educational policy relate incidental reports about tensions in classes with an ethnically heterogeneous pupil population predominantly to safety issues and the problems of immigrant youth. This socio-political climate might threaten ethnic-cultural relations in Dutch society and is an impediment to a positive and inclusive learning environment for the immigrant youth. With the help of a survey we asked teachers of ethnically diverse classes about their experiences and perceptions. Like the teachers in Leeman's interview study, they present a different picture. The teachers do state that they have experienced tensions in the contact between themselves and their pupils but scarcely relate these situations to the ethnically heterogeneous pupil population. This is an interesting outcome that gives an indication of the incompatibility in the Netherlands between the debate on education and teachers' actual experiences.

The teachers in the survey did relate the tensions to the ethnic mix when they experienced them in class discussions about cultural and religious issues. However, less than half the teachers experienced such situations. When they do, they find them among the most stressful and difficult to decide how to react to.

We selected twenty situations in which teachers could possibly experience a diversity of value dilemmas that could be related to ethnic diversity. Nineteen situations proved to be relevant. None of the 87 teachers added a new type of situation. The experiences of teachers with tense situations scarcely differed by personal and context characteristics. But the teachers who are more interculturally sensitive – in this study assessed according to how much they value the ethnically heterogeneous pupil population – experienced fewer situations in total and five situations less frequently that reflected the whole range of diversity we presented to them. These teachers

194

might be good at creating a pleasant social climate in the class and because of their positive attitude towards ethnic-cultural diversity may experience fewer tensions. This is in line with an observation made by a teacher from a Moluccan background interviewed by Leeman:

> Many of my colleagues generalise and have difficulty in seeing the pupil as an individual. They don't make enough effort to create a relationship of trust with pupils. They feel a distance between them and their Moroccan pupils and make fools of them. Those teachers experience such things as being spat at in the face, pupils not accepting the authority of women teachers, and pupils putting themselves at a distance. They exaggerate incidents out of all proportion. (2006:352)

Another possibility is that they regard an ethnically diverse context as an educational resource and perceive these situations as normal in the teaching context; they do not associate them with the questions we asked, in which we relate them to tension and difficulties (Henze *et al*, 2000).

At the beginning of this chapter we stated that noticing tense situations and reacting to them are important teaching competences in ethnically heterogeneous classes. After noticing the situations, teachers can assess them in many different ways, for example, as an expression of problem behaviour by the pupil or as an indication of inadequate inclusion of diversity in the class, school and society. Broader social issues frequently intersect with classroom issues. Teachers of ethnically heterogeneous classes should be aware of the cultural and moral dimensions of teaching and should be alert to their own role regarding social justice and cultural diversity (Mason, 2002; Moore, 2004; Leeman and Reid, 2006). Their professionalism is at stake.

The teachers in this study proved to be willing to take action and to react, generally by discussing the situations with pupils. These teachers seem to prefer a democratic way of dealing with tensions. Dialogue is also preferable from the perspective of social justice and intercultural education. However, the survey gives no insight into whether teachers are focusing on intercultural education during class discussions, nor into how their actions and behaviour work in practice in the classroom. Moreover, it was the tensions that teachers experienced during class discussions that they found difficult to react to. The ability of teachers to guide class discussions on cultural and religious issues should be the theme of further research and the professionalisation of teachers.

Note
The Netherlands Organisation for Scientific Research financed this project. The authors hold full responsibility for the text.

References

Ahmed, S. (1997) 'It's a Sun-tan, isn't it?' Autobiography as an Identificatory Practice' in H. Mirza (ed) *Black British Feminism: A Reader.* London/New York: Routledge

Ålund, A. (1997) *Multikultiungdom. Kön, etnicitet, identitet.* [Multicultural youth. Gender, ethnicity, identity] Lund: Pupillitteratur

Anthias, F. and Yuval-Davis, N. (1992) *Racialised Boundaries: Race, Nation, Gender, Colour and Class and the Anti-Racist Struggle.* London: Routledge

Anzaldua, G. (1987) *Borderlands/La Frontera: The New Mestiza.* San Francisco, California: Aunt Lute Books

Arendt, H. (1958) *The Human Condition.* London and Chicago: University of Chicago Press

Arendt, H. (1963) *On Revolution.* London: Penguin

Aspinall. P. (2003) The conceptualisation and categorisation of mixed race/ethnicity in Britain and North America: Identity options and the role of the state. *International Journal of Intercultural Relations,* 27(3)

Barany, Z. (2000) The socio-economic impact of regime change in Eastern Europe: Gypsy marginality in the 1990s. *East European Politics and Societies,* 14(2)

Barth, F. (Ed) (1969) *Ethnic Groups and Boundaries: the Social Organisation of Culture Difference.* Oslo: Universitetsforlaget

Basit, T.N., Roberts, L., McNamara, O., Carrington, B., Maguire, M. and Woodrow, D. (2006) Did they jump or were they pushed? Reasons why minority ethnic teachers withdraw from Initial Teacher Training courses, *British Educational Research Journal,* 32(3)

Batelaan, P. ed (1998) *Towards an equitable classroom. Cooperative Learning in Education.* Hiversum: IAIE

Batelaan, P., Van Hoof C. (1996) Cooperative learning in intercultural education. *European Journal of Intercultural Studies,* 7(3)

Bauman, Z. (2003) *Intervista sull'identità.* Bari: Editori Laterza

Beck, E. (1999) Language rights and Turkish children in Germany. *Patterns of Prejudice,* 33(2)

Beck, U. and Beck-Gernsheim, E. (2001) *Individualisation: Institutionalised Individualism and its Social and Political Consequences.* London: Sage

Beck, U. (2006) *Cosmopolitan Vision*. Cambridge: Polity Press

Beijaard D., Meijer P.C., and Verloop N. (2004) Reconsidering research on teachers' professional identity, *Teaching and Teacher Education* 20(2)

Bhatti, G. (1999) Asian Children at Home and at School: an Ethnographic Study. London: Routledge

Bhatti, G. (2001) Social Justice, Education and Inclusion, *The School Field*, 12(3/4)

Bhatti, G. (2003) Social Justice and Non-Traditional Participants in Higher Education: a tale of 'border-crossing', instrumentalism and drift in: C. Vincent (ed) *Social Justice, Education and Identity*. London: Routledge

Bhatti, G. (2004) Good, Bad and Normal Teachers: the experiences of South Asian Children, in: G.L.Billings and D. Gillborn (eds) *The Routledge Falmer Reader in Multicultural Education*. London: Routledge

Bhopal, K. , Gundara, J., Jones, C. and Owen, C. (2000) *Working Towards Inclusive Education for Gypsy Traveller Pupils* (RR 238). London: DfEE

Biggs, J. (1987) *Student Approaches to learning and Studying*. Hawthorn AU: Australian Council for Educational Research

Boulton-Lewis, G.M., Smith, D.J.H., McCrindle, A.R., Burnett, P.C. and Campbell, K.J. (2001) Secondary Teachers' conceptions of Teaching and Learning. *Learning and Instruction*, 36(1)

Brookfield S. (1990) Using critical incidents to explore assumptions, Mezirow J. and Associates, *Fostering critical reflection in adulthood: a guide to transformative and emancipatory learning*. San Francisco: Jossey-Bass

Brookfield, S. (1995) Tales from the dark side: a phenomenography of adult critical reflection, *International Journal of Lifelong Education*, 13(3)

Bruner, J. (1998) *Uddanelseskulturen*. Copenhagen: Munksgaard

Burbules, N.C. and Bruce, B.C. (2001) Theory and research on teaching as dialogue. In: Richardson, V. (Ed.) *Handbook of Research on Teaching*. Washington: AERA

Burr, V. (1995) *An Introduction to Social Constructionism*. London: Routledge

Carli, B. (2004) *The Making and Breaking of a Female Culture: The History of Swedish Physical Education in a Different Voice*. Göteborg, Acta Universitatis Gothoburgensis

Central Statistics Office (CSO) (2005) *Population and Labour Force Projections 2006-2036*. Dublin: the Stationery Office

Chen, G.M. and Starosta, W.J. (2000) *The development and validation of the Intercultural Sensitivity Scale*. Paper presented at the annual meeting of National Communication Association, Seattle

Clarke, M. and Drudy, S. (2006) Teaching for diversity, social justice and global awareness. *European Journal of Teacher Education*, 29(3)

Cochran-Smith, M. (1995) Color blindness and basket making are not the answers: confronting the dilemmas of race, culture and language diversity in teacher education, *American Educational Research Journal*, 32(3)

Cockrell, P.L., Cockrell, D.H. and Middleton, J.N. (1999) Coming to terms with 'diversity' and 'multiculturalism' in teacher education: Learning about our students, changing our practice. *Teaching and Teacher Education* 15(4)

Cohen, E.G. (1994) *Designing Groupwork. Strategies for the Heterogeneous Classroom.* New York: Teachers College Press

Cohen E.G. (2003) *Equità, scuola e Istruzione Complessa: i principi di base, in Gobbo, F. (a cura di) Multiculturalismo e intercultura.* Padua: IMPRIMITUR Editrice

Cohen, E.G., Lotan R. eds (1997). *Working for Equity in Heterogeneous Classrooms. Sociological Theory in Practice.* New York: Teachers College Press

Colley, H. and Hodkinson, P. (2001) 'Problems with Bridging the Gap: the reversal of structure and agency in addressing social exclusion', *Critical Social Policy* 21(3)

Connell, R.W. (1996a) *Maskuliniteter.* [Masculinities] Göteborg: Daidalos

Connell, R.W. (1996b) Teaching the Boys: New Research on Masculinity, and Gender Strategies for school. *Teachers College Records*, 98(2)

Cordingley, P. (1999) Constructing and critiquing reflective practice. *Educational Action Research*, 7(2)

Cork. L. (2005) *Supporting Black Pupils and Parents: Understanding and Improving home-school relations.* London: Routledge

Council of Europe (CoE) (1993, 1995) *The city's approach to the education of its multicultural population (migrants and minorities).* Paper presented at the Amsterdam seminar of the standing conference of local and regional authorities, Amsterdam, The Netherlands. Strasbourg: Council of Europe

Council of Europe (CoE) (2001) *Second report on Germany* (Report No. CRI(2001)36). Strasbourg: European Committee against Racism and Intolerance

Crowe, D. M. (2003) The international and historical dimensions of Romani migration in Central and Eastern Europe. *Nationalities Papers*, 31(1)

Croxford, L.(2000a) Inequality in Attainment at Age 16: A 'Home International' Comparison, *CES Briefing No. 19.* Edinburgh: Centre for Educational Sociology, University of Edinburgh

Croxford, L. (2000b) Gender and national curricula, in J. Salisbury and S. Riddell (eds) *Gender, Policy and Educational Change.* London: Routledge

Croxford, L. (2006) The Youth Cohort Surveys – how good is the evidence? *CES Briefing No 38.* Edinburgh: Centre for Educational Sociology, University of Edinburgh

Croxford, L. and Paterson, L. (forthcoming) Trends in social class segregation between schools in England, Wales and Scotland since 1984. *Research Papers in Education*

Delamont, S. (2001) *Changing women, unchanged men?* Buckingham: Open University Press

Derrington, C. and Kendall, S. (2004) *Gypsy Traveller Students in Secondary Schools: Culture, Identity and Achievement.* Stoke-on-Trent: Trentham Books.

Desforges, C. (1995). How does experience affect theoretical knowledge for teaching? *Learning and Instruction,* 5(4)

Domínguez, S. P. (1999) Teachers' attitudes about the integration of Roma: the case of Spain. *European Journal of Intercultural Studies,* 10(2)

Drudy, S., Martin, M., Woods, M. and O'Flynn, J. (2005) *Men and the classroom: gender imbalances in teaching,* London: RoutledgeFalmer.

Epstein, D. (1999) Real boys don't work: 'underachievement', masculinity and the harassment of 'sissies'. In D Epstein, J Elwood, V Hey and J Man (Eds), *Failing boys? Issues in gender and achievement.* Buckingham: Open University Press

European Monitoring Centre on Racism and Xenophobia, Raxen 3 (2002) Annual Report, *Analytical study on legislation: report on Ireland,* http://www.nccri.ie/pdf/legislation_Raxen.3pdf (last accessed on 21 July 2006)

EU Monitoring and Advocacy Program (EUMAP) (2002) *Monitoring the EU accession process: Minority protection. Volume II: Case studies in selected member states. France, Germany, Italy, Spain, United Kingdom.* Budapest, Hungary: Open Society Institute

Equality Authority (2006) *Annual Report 2005.* Dublin: Equality Authority

Florio-Ruane, S. (1996) *La cultura e l'organizzazione sociale della classe scolastica, in Gobbo, F. (a cura di), Antropologia dell'educazione. Scuola, cultura, educazione nella società multiculturale.* Milan: Edizioni Unicopli

Foucault, M. (1972) *The Archaeology of Knowledge.* London: Tavistock

Foucault, M. (1979) *Discipline and Punish: The Birth of the Prison.* Harmondsworth: Penguin

Frankenberg, R. (1993) *White Women, Race Matters: The Social Construction of Whiteness.* Minneapolis: University of Minnesota Press

Fraser, N. (1997) *Justice Interruptus.* London: Routledge

Frosh, S., Phoenix, A. and Pattman, R. (2002) *Young Masculinities.* New York: Palgrave

Gaine, C. (2005) *We're All White, Thanks.* Stoke on Trent: Trentham Books

Garrett Dikkers, A. (2006) *Education of Roma children in Germany: Choosing among alternative programs.* (Doctoral dissertation, University of Minnesota, 2006)

Gerwirtz, S. 1998) Conceptualising Social Justice in education: mapping the territory, *Journal of Education Policy,* 13(4)

Gillborn, D. and Youdell, D. (1999) *Rationing Education.* Buckingham: Open University Press

Gitz-Johansen, T. (2003) Representations of ethnicity: How teachers speak about ethnic minority students. In D Beach, T Gordon and E Lahelma (Eds) *Democratic education: Ethnographic challenges.* London: Tufnell Press

Gobbo, F. (2000) *Pedagogia interculturale. Il progetto educativo nelle società complesse.* Rome: Carocci

Gobbo, F. (2003) C'è una giostra nel futuro? Esperienza scolastica e processo di inculturazione in una minoranza occupazionale nomade, in Gobbo, F. (a cura di) *Etnografia dell'educazione in Europa. Soggetti, contesti, questioni metodologiche*, Milan: Edizioni Unicopli

Gobbo, F. (2004) Cultural Intersections: the life story of a Roma cultural mediator. *European Educational Research Journal*, 3(3)

Gobbo, F. (2006) Along the Margins, Across the Borders: Teaching and Learning among Vento attrazionisti viaggianti, in Antelitz, Coombes P., Danaher P. eds., Marginalised pedagogues? International Studies of the Work and Identities of Contemporary Educators Teaching 'Minority' Learners, special issue of *Teaching and Teacher Education*, 22 (7)

Gobbo, F. (2007) Between the road and the town: the education of travelling attractionists. An ethnographic research, in Pink W. T., Noblit G. W. eds., *International Handbook of Urban Education*. Dordrecht: Springer (in press)

Gobbo, F., Traversi, M., Augelli, A. (2005) Cooperative Learning nelle classi multiculturali. *Educazione interculturale*, 3(1)

Gordon, L.R. (1995) Critical 'mixed race?' *Social Identities*, 1(3)

Gordon, J. (2000) *The Colour of Teaching*. Buckingham:Open University Press

Gordon, T., Holland, J. and Lahelma, E. (2000) Friends or foes? Interpreting relations between girls in school. In G. Walford and C. Hudson (Eds) *Genders and sexualities in educational ethnography* (3). Amsterdam: JAI, Elsevier Science

Gow, L. and McPherson, A. (1980) *Tell Them From Me: Scottish school leavers write about school and life afterwards*. Aberdeen: Aberdeen University Press

Greene, M. (1995) *Releasing the Imagination: Essays on Education, the Arts, and Social Change*. San Francisco: Jossey Bass

Griffiths, M. (2003) *Action for Social Justice in Education: Fairly Different*. Buckingham: Open University Press

Grimmett, P. P. Erickson, G. L. Mackinnon, A. M. and Riecken, T. J. (1990) Reflective practice in teacher education, in Clift, R. Thouston, W. R. and Pugach, M. C. (eds) *Encouraging reflective practice in education*, pp20-38, New York: Teachers College Press

Halsey, A. H. (2000) 'A Hundred Years of Social Change', *Social Trends* 30 www.statistics.gov.uk/downloads/theme_social/st30v8.pdf

Hancock, I. (1997) The Struggle for the Control of Identity. *Patrin Web Journal* 4(4)

Hansen, D.T. (2001) Teaching as a moral activity. In V. Richardson (Ed.) *Handbook of Research on Teaching*. Washington: AERA

Hansen, E.J. (1995) *En generation blev voksen. Rapport 95:8*. Copenhagen: Socialforskningsinstituttet

Henze, R., Katz, A. and Norte, E. (2000) Rethinking the concept of racial or ethnic conflict in schools: a leadership perspective. *Race, Ethnicity and Education*, 3(2)

Holden, C. (2003) Education for global citizenship: the knowledge, understanding and motivation of trainee teachers, Ross, A (ed), *A Europe of many cultures: Proceedings of the fifth conference of the children's identity and citizenship in Europe thematic network* CiCe, London, 361-367

Homan, M. (2006) *Generatie Lonsdale. Extreem rechtse jongeren in Nederland na Fortuyn en Van Gogh. [The Lonsdale generation. Extreme right youngsters in the Netherlands since Fortuyn and Van Gogh.]* Antwerp/Amsterdam: Houtekiet

Hoodless, P. (2004) Are you just helping? The perceptions and experiences of minority ethnic trainees on a one-year primary Initial Teacher Training Course, *Research in Education*, 72( )

Huber, G.L., Sorrentino, R.M., Eppler Davidson, M. and Roth, M.H.J. (1992) Uncertainty orientation and co-operative learning: Individual differences within and across cultures. *Learning and Individual Differences*, 4(1)

Husu, J. (2002) *Representing the practice of teachers' pedagogical knowing.* Turku: Finnish Educational Research Association

Ifekwunigwe, J.O. (1999) *Scattered Belongings: Cultural Paradoxes of 'Race', Nation and Gender.* London; New York: Routledge

Jones, C. Maguire, M. and Watson, B. (1997) The School Experiences of Some Minority Ethnic Students in London Schools during Teacher Training, *Journal of Education for Teaching*, 23(2)

Jenkins, R. (2004) *Social Identity.* London: Routledge

Kendrick, D. and Bakewell, S. (1995) *On the Verge: the Gypsies of England.* University of Hertfordshire Press.

Klaassen, C. and Leeferink, H. (1998) *Partners in opvoeding in het basisonderwijs: ouders en docenten over de pedagogische opdracht en de afstemming tussen gezin en school.* [Partners in upbringing in primary education: parents and teachers on the moral task of education and the interaction between family and school.] Assen: Van Gorcum

Kleijer, H., Van Reekum, R. and Tillekens, G. (2004) *Respect! De alledaagse werkelijkheid van het 'zwarte' vmbo.* [Respect! The daily reality of the 'black' pre-vocational school.] Sociologische Gids, 51(2)

Klopp, B. (2002) *German multiculturalism: Immigrant integration and the transformation of citizenship.* Westport, CT: Praeger Publishers

Leach, C.(1994) Managing whole – school change, in Osler, A. (ed) *Development education: global perspectives in the curriculum.* London: Cassell

Leeman, Y. (2006) Teaching in ethnically diverse schools: teachers' professionalism. *European Journal of Teacher Education*, 29(3)

Leeman, Y. and Pels, T. (2006) Citizenship Education in the Dutch Multiethnic Context. *European Education*, 38(2)

Leeman, Y. and Reid, C. (2006) Multi/intercultural education in Australia and the Netherlands. *Compare*, 36(1)

Leidgeb, F. and Horn, N. (1994) *Opre Roma! Erhebt euch! Eine Einführung in die Geschichte und Situation der Roma.* Munich, Germany: AG Spak Bücher

Liégeois, J.-P. (1989) *Gypsy children in school: Training for teachers and other personnel* (Summer University organised by the Centre de recherches tsiganes, Montauban Teachers' Training College, France, 4-8 July 1988 No. DECS/EGT (88) 42). Strasbourg: Council of Europe

Liégeois, J.-P. (1999) School provision for Roma children: A European perspective. *European Journal of Intercultural Studies*, 10(2)

Lindblad, S. and Popkewitz, T. (eds) (1999) Education Governance and Social Integration and Exclusion: national cases of education systems and recent reforms, *Uppsala Reports on Education* 34. Uppsala: Universitetstryckeriet

Lindemann, F. (2005) *Schule muss schmecken! Ermutigende Erfahrungen junger Roma in deutschen Bildungswesen*. Hernsbach, Germany: Beltz Verlag

Lloyd, G., Stead, J., Jordan, E. and Norris, C. (1999) Teachers and Gypsy Travellers. *Scottish Educational Review*. 31.

Lotan, R.A. (2003) Group-worthy tasks, in *Educational Leadership*, 6 (6)

Lotan, R.A. (2006a) Managing groupwork, in Evertson, C. and C. Weinstein (eds.) *Handbook of Classroom Management: Research, Practice, and Contemporary Issues*. New Jersey: Lawrence Erlbaum Associates

Lotan, R.A. (2006b) Teaching teachers to build equitable classrooms. *Theory into Practice*, 45(1)

Lynch, K. and Lodge, A. (2002) *Equality and power in schools: Redistribution, Recognition and Representation*. London and New York: RoutledgeFalmer

Lyotard, J-F. (1984) *The Postmodern Condition: A Report on Knowledge*. Trans. Geoff Bennington and Brian Massumi. Manchester: Manchester University Press

Lyotard, J-F. (1989) *The Differend: Phrases in Dispute*. Trans. George Van Den Abbeele. Minneapolis: University of Minnesota Press

Mac an Ghaill, M. (1988) *Young, Gifted and Black*. Milton Keyes: Open University Press

Mac an Ghaill, M. (1994) *The making of men. Masculinities, sexualities and schooling*. Buckingham: Open University Press

Mahtani, M. (2002) 'What's in a name?' *Ethnicities* 2(4)

Marton, F. and Saljö, R. (1979) *Learning in the learner's perspective 3. Level of difficulty seen as a relationship between the reader and the text*. Göteborg Universitet: Pedagogiska Institutionen

Marton, F., Dall'Alba, G. and Beaty, E. (1993) Conceptions of Learning. *International Journal of Educational Research*, 19(3)

Marton, F. and Booth, S. (1997) *Learning and Awareness*. Mahwah, New Jersey: Lawrence Erlbaum

Maslovaty, N. (2000) Teachers' choice of teaching strategies for dealing with socio-moral dilemmas in the elementary school. *Journal of Moral Education*, 29(4)

Mason, J. (2002). *Researching your own practice. The discipline of noticing*. London/New York: Routledge-Falmer

Mayring, P. (2000) Qualitative Content Analysis Forum: *Qualitative Social Research*, 1(2) http://www.qualitative-research.net/fqs-texte/2-00/2-00mayring-e.htm (last accessed 13 July 2006)

McEachron, G and Bhatti G. (2005) Language Support for Immigrant Children-a study of state schools in UK and US, *Language, Culture and Curriculum*, 18(2)

McPherson, A. and Willms, J. D. (1987) Equalisation and improvement: some effects of comprehensive reorganisation in Scotland, *Sociology*, 21(4)

McPherson of Cluny, Sir W. (1999) *The Stephen Lawrence Inquiry: Report of an Inquiry by Sir William Mc Pherson of Cluny*. London: HMSO

Minguez , M.L.G. and Murillo, J. (1996) Reforms of Compulsory Education in Europe (1984-1994), *EERA Bulletin*, 2(3)

Ministerie van Onderwijs Cultuur en Wetenschappen (2004) *Onderwijs, Integratie en Burgerschap*. [Education, integration and citizenship] Brief dd 23-4-2004 aan de Tweede Kamer der Staten Generaal

Mirga, A., and Cheorghe, N. (1997) *The Roma in the 21st century*. Retrieved August 24, 2004, from http://www.per-usa.org/21st_c.htm

Mitchel, C. and Weber, S. (1996) *Reinventing ourselves as teachers: private and social acts as Memory and Imagination*. London: Falmer

Modood, T. (1992) *Not Easy Being British*. Stoke on Trent: Trentham Books

Modood, T., Beishon, S. and Virdee, S. (1994) *Changing Ethnic Identities*. London: Policy Studies Institute

Modood, T., Berthoud, R., Lakey, J., Smith, P., Virdee, S. and Beishon, S. (1997) *Ethnic Minorities in Britain*. London: Policy Studies Institute

Moore, A. (2004) *The good teacher. Dominant discourses in teaching and teacher education*. London/New York: Routledge-Falmer

Munby, H. and Russell, T. (1993) Reflective teacher education: technique or epistemology, *Teaching and Teacher Education*, 9(4)

National Focal Point of the European Monitoring Centre on Racism and Xenophobia (2002) *Analytical Study on Legislation: Report on Ireland*

Newman, S. (1999) Constructing and critiquing reflective practice [1] in *Educational Action Research*, 7(1)

Novak, M. (2000) Defining social justice, *First Things* 108

Nussbaum, M. (2003) Capabilities as fundamental entitlements: Sen and social justice, *Feminist Economics* 9 (2-3)

Oakeshott, M. (1962) The Voice of Poetry in the Conversation of Mankind, *Rationalism in Politics and Other Essays*. London: Methuen

Office for Standards in Education (1996) *The Education of Travelling Children*. London: Ofsted

Office for Standards in Education (1999) *Raising the Attainment of Ethnic Minority Pupils*. London: Ofsted

Office for Standards in Education (2003) *Provision and Support for Traveller Pupils*. London: Ofsted

Öhrn, E. (2000) Contemporary Swedish research and debate on gender and education. *Nora*, 8(3)

Öhrn, E. (2002) Jämställdhet som en del av skolans värdegrund. Om kön, klass och etnicitet i skolvardagen. [Gender equality as part of the school's fundamental values. On gender, class and ethnicity in everyday schooling] In G-M. Frånberg and D. Kallós (Eds), *Demokrati i skolans vardag. Fem nordiska forskare rapporterar*. Värdegrundscentrum, Umeå universitet för NSS, Nordiska Ministerrådet

Öhrn, E. (2005) *Att göra skillnad. En studie av ungdomar som politiska aktörer i skolans vardag.* [To make a difference. A study of young people as political actors in school]. Report no 2005:07, Göteborg University: Department of Education

Osbeck, C., Holm, A-S. and Wernersson, I. (2003) *Kränkningar i skolan. Förekomst, former och sammanhang.* [Offences in school.] Göteborg: Värdegrunden

Organisation for Security and Cooperation in Europe (2003) *Action plan on improving the situation of Roma and Sinti within the OSCE area.* Vienna: OSCE

Oser, F. (1991) Professional morality: a discourse approach. In: Kurtines, W. and Gewirtz, J. (Eds.) *Handbook of moral behavior and development.* New Jersey: Lawrence Erlbaum Association

Oser, F. and Althof, W. (1993) Trust in advance: on the professional morality of teachers. *Journal of Moral Education*, 22(3)

Osler, A. (1994) Education for Democracy and equality- the experiences , values and attitudes of ethnic minority student teachers, *European Journal of Intercultural Studies*, 5(1)

Osler, A. (1997) *The Education and Careers of Black Teachers: changing identities, changing lives.* Buckingham: Open University Press

Ozga, J. and Lawn, M. (1999) The cases of England and Scotland within the United Kingdom, in Lindblad, S and Popkewitz, T (eds) Education Governance and Social Integration and Exclusion : national cases of education systems and recent reforms, *Uppsala Reports on Education* 34. Uppsala: Universitetstryckeriet

Paccione, A.V. (2000) Developing a commitment to multicultural education. *Teachers College Record*, 102(6)

Paechter, C. and Head, J. (1996) Gender, Identity, Status and the body: life in a marginal subject. *Gender and Education*, 8(1)

Palermo, J. (2003) Reading Lyotard, on the Politics of the New. *Philosophy of Education Yearbook* 373-375

Parker, D. and Song, M. (2001) 'Introduction: Rethinking 'mixed race'' in D. Parker and M. Song (eds) *Rethinking Mixed Race.* London: Pluto

Parker, W.C. (2003) Can we talk? In: Parker, W.C. *Teaching Democracy: unity and diversity in public life.* New York, Teachers College Press

Perkins, J. (1999) Continuity in German history? The treatment of the Gypsies. *Immigrants and Minorities*, 18(1)

Phelan, A. (1997) When the mirror crack'd: the discourse of reflection in pre-service teacher education in Watson, K., Modgil, C. and Modgil, S. (eds) *Educational Dilemmas: Debate and Diversity,* volume one, *Teachers, Teacher Education and Training.* London: Cassell

Phoenix, A. (2004) Using informal pedagogy to oppress themselves and each other. Critical pedagogy, schooling and 11-14 year old London boys. *Nordisk Pedagogik* 24(1)

Powney, J, Wilson, V, Hall, S. Davidson, J. Kirk, S. Edward, S, Mirza, H. (2003) *Teachers' Careers: the Impact of Age, Disability, Ethnicity, Gender and Sexual*

Orientation, Research Report 488, SCRE Centre, University of Glasgow and CRES: Middlesex University, Department for Education and Skills

Raffe, D., Brannen. K., Croxford, L. and Martin, C. (1999) Comparing England, Scotland, Wales and Northern Ireland: the case for 'home internationals' in comparative research, *Comparative Education*, 35(1)

Reay, D. (1997) The double-bind of the 'working class' feminist academic: the failure of success or the success of failure in: C. Zmroczek, and P. Mahony (eds) *Class matters: working class women's perspectives on social class.* London: Taylor and Francis

Reeves, F. (1983) *British Racial Discourse: a Study of British Political Discourse About Race and Race-Related Matters.* Cambridge: Cambridge University Press

Rego Santos, M.A. and Nieto, S.. (2000) Multicultural/intercultural teacher education in two contexts: lessons from the United States and Spain, *Teaching and Teacher Education* 16(4)

Runnymede Trust (2000) *The Future of Multi-Ethnic Britain.* (The Parekh Report). London: Profile Books

Ringold, D., Orenstein, M. A., and Wilkens, E. (2005) *Roma in an expanding Europe: Breaking the poverty cycle.* Washington: World Bank

Ringold, D. (2000) *Roma and the transition in Central and Eastern Europe: Trends and challenges.* Washington: World Bank

Rogers, E. (1995) *Diffusion of innovations.* New York: Free Press

Root, M. (ed) (1992) *Racially Mixed People in America.* Newbury Park, California: Sage

Root, M. (1996) 'The Multiracial Experience: Racial Borders as Significant Frontier in Race Relations' in M. Root (ed) *The Multiracial Experience: Racial Borders as the New Frontier.* Thousand Oaks, California: Sage

Saljö, R. (1979 a) *Learning in the Learner's Perspective 1. Some common-sense conceptions.* Göteborg Univewrsitet: Pedagogiska Institutionen

Saljö, R. (1979 b) *Learning in the Learner's Perspective 2. Differences in awareness.* Göteborg Universitet: Pedagogiska Institutionen

Saljö, R. (1979c) *Learning in the Learners's Perspective 4. Considering one's own strategy.* Göteborg Universitet: Pedagogiska Institutionen

Sarantakos, S. (1993) *Social Research.* Sydney: Macmillan Education Australia

Schermerhorn, R. (1970) *Comparative Ethnic Relations.* New York: Random House

Schön, D. A. (1983) *The Reflective Practitioner: how professionals think in action.* New York: Basic Books

Sen, A. (2002) Response to Commentaries, *Studies in Comparative International development* 37(2)

Serafini, F. (2001) Three paradigms of assessment: measurement, procedure, and inquiry, *The Reading Teacher*, 54(4)

Serafini, F. (2003) Dimensions of reflective practice, http://serafini.nevada.edu/Handouts/ReflectivePractice.htm (last accessed November 2005)

Sernhede, O. (2002) *Alie-Nation is My Nation. Hiphop och unga mäns utan-förskap i Det Nya Sverige.* [Alie-Nation is My Nation. Hiphop and youth men's alienation in The new Sweden]. Stockholm: Ordfronts förlag

Sernhede, O. (in press) Urbanization of injustice, immigrant youth and informal schooling. In A Luke and W Pink (Eds), *International Handbook of Urban Education.* Dordrecht: Springer

Sewell, T. (1997) *Black Masculinities and Schooling – how black boys survive modern schooling.* Stoke-on-Trent: Trentham

Shannon, P. and Crawford, P. (1998) 'Summers off' representation of teachers' work and other discontents, *Language Arts* 74(4)

Skinner, D. (2004) 'Racialised futures: biologism and the changing politics of identity'. Paper presented at British Sociological Association Annual Conference, University of York, March 2004

Sleeter, C.E. (1993) How White Teachers Construct Race in: C. McCarthy and W. Crichlow (eds) *Race, Identity and Representation in Education.* New York: Routledge

Smith, J. and Osborn, M. (2003) Interpretative phenomenological analysis in J. Smith (ed) *Qualitative Psychology: A practical guide to research methods.* London: Sage

Smith, R and Zantiotis R (1989). Practical teacher education and the avante garde, in Giroux, H. and McLaren, P. (eds) *Critical Pedagogy, the State and Cultural Struggle,* New York: State University of New York

Smith, T. (1997) Recognising difference: The Romani 'Gypsy' child socialisation and education process. *British Journal of Sociology of Education,* 18(2)

Stemler, S. (2001) *Practical assessment, research and evaluation,* 7 (17), http://PAREonline.net/getvn.asp?v=7&n=17 (last accessed 13 July 2006)

Sullivan, C. (1993) View Points Oppression: the experiences of a lesbian teacher in an inner city comprehensive school in the United Kingdom. *Gender and Education,* 5(1)

Tabachnick, B. R. and Zeichner, K. M. (eds) (1991) *Issues and Practices in Inquiry-Oriented Teacher Education.* London: Falmer

Tessman, L. (1999) The racial politics of mixed race. *Journal of Social Philosophy,* 30(2)

Tirri, K. (1999) Teachers' perceptions of moral dilemmas at school. *Journal of Moral Education,* 28(1)

Veugelers, W. and De Kat, E. (1998) *Opvoeden in het voortgezet onderwijs: leerlingen, ouders en docenten over de pedagogische opdracht en de afstemming tussen gezin en school.*[Upbringing in secondary education: pupils, parents and teachers on the moral task of education and the interaction between family and school.] Assen: Van Gorcum

Villegas, A.M. and Lucas, T. (2002) Preparing culturally responsive teachers. Rethinking the curriculum. *Journal of Teacher Education,* 53(1)

Wal, J. ter (2004) *European Day of Media Monitoring: Quantitative analysis of daily press and TV contents in the 15 EU Member States* (No. Online/More

Colour in the Media): European Research Centre on Migration and Ethnic Relations

Walker, V.S. and Snarey, J.R. (2004) *Race-ing Moral Formation: African-American perspectives on care and justice.* New York: Teachers College Press

Wenger, E. (1998) *Communities of Practice-learning, Meaning and Identity.* Cambridge: Cambridge University Press

Woods, P. (1983) Coping at School through Humour, *British Journal of Sociology of Education,* 4(2)

Young, I. M. (1990) *Justice and the Politics of Difference.* Princeton: Princeton University Press

Yuen, Y. K. J. Y. S. (2000) Prevention of discrimination against and the protection of minorities: The human rights problems and protection of the Roma (Working paper). UN Economic and Social Council

Zeichner, K (2001) Connecting genuine teacher development to the struggle for social justice A revised version of a lecture given in July 1991 at the Institute in Teacher Education, Simon Fraser University, Burnaby, British Columbia, Canada, http://ncrtl.msu.edu/http/ipapers/html/pdf/ip921.pdf (last accessed 6th July 2006)

Index